ISBN 978-1-330-35362-2
PIBN 10038038

This book is a reproduction of an important historical work. Forgotten Books uses
state-of-the-art technology to digitally reconstruct the work, preserving the original format
whilst repairing imperfections present in the aged copy. In rare cases, an imperfection in
the original, such as a blemish or missing page, may be replicated in our edition. We do,
however, repair the vast majority of imperfections successfully; any imperfections that
remain are intentionally left to preserve the state of such historical works.

1 MONTH OF
FREE
READING

at

www.ForgottenBooks.com

By purchasing this book you are eligible for one month membership to ForgottenBooks.com, giving you unlimited access to our entire collection of over 700,000 titles via our web site and mobile apps.

To claim your free month visit:
www.forgottenbooks.com/free38038

English
Français
Deutsche
Italiano
Español
Português

www.forgottenbooks.com

Mythology Photography **Fiction**
Fishing Christianity **Art** Cooking
Essays Buddhism Freemasonry
Medicine **Biology** Music **Ancient**
Egypt Evolution Carpentry Physics
Dance Geology **Mathematics** Fitness
Shakespeare **Folklore** Yoga Marketing
Confidence Immortality Biographies
Poetry **Psychology** Witchcraft
Electronics Chemistry History **Law**
Accounting **Philosophy** Anthropology
Alchemy Drama Quantum Mechanics
Atheism Sexual Health **Ancient History**
Entrepreneurship Languages Sport
Paleontology Needlework Islam
Metaphysics Investment Archaeology
Parenting Statistics Criminology
Motivational

Miss Julie H. Biddell.

With the

Kindest good wishes

of

R. F. Meysey - Thompson.

A HUNTING CATECHISM

A HUNTING CATECHISM

BY

COLONEL R. F. MEYSEY-THOMPSON

AUTHOR OF "A FISHING CATECHISM," "A SHOOTING CATECHISM,"
"REMINISCENCES OF THE COURT, THE CAMP, AND THE
CHASE," ETC.

LONDON

EDWARD ARNOLD

41 & 43, MADDOX STREET, BOND STREET, W.

1907

PREFACE

THIS little Catechism on Hunting is intended for the use of beginners, like its predecessors on Fishing and Shooting, and was suggested by the instructions given to my own children from past experience. That experience has been a wide one. Just forty-one years ago, at the age of nineteen, I joined the Rifle Brigade, and bought my first horse for a very modest sum; and I have never been without a horse since that time.

An allowance of £200 per annum, in addition to a subaltern's pay, out of which all regimental subscriptions to mess and band funds had to be paid, besides travelling expenses, and the cost of keeping up an expensive uniform, with private clothes, did not afford much margin for buying a horse and then keeping it. I did not therefore venture on the expense of a groom, but essayed to manage for the horse myself, with the assistance of my soldier servant, whose only qualification for the task was that he had been in the Camel Corps in the Indian Mutiny! No sooner did the horse arrive than we were in difficulties at once, and I found the one of us knew about as much, or rather as little, as the other. However, we managed somehow, and the pleasure I got out of my horse was immense.

Realising that I knew absolutely nothing about horses, and that, if they did not pay for themselves, I certainly could not do so, and casting about for a means of improving my knowledge, I was fortunate in finding in the mess a copy of " Youatt on the Horse," then a comparatively new work. I learned this almost by heart, and taking each part of the anatomy in succession, after carefully studying what the book said, I sallied into the streets to search for examples, which were found chiefly in the cab-ranks ; and the knowledge thus gained proved as great a power as real knowledge always does.

Race-riding, hunting, and training followed in due course, and having been my own purchaser, breaker, groom, trainer, jockey, and veterinary surgeon, with satisfactory results, I have necessarily tried innumerable ways, systems, and recipes, some of which, though they may have been fairly successful, have been at once discarded, when I have been convinced another was better, though I have held firmly to what has been proved to be sound, heedless of the passing whims of fashion.

My grateful thanks are here proffered to Tom Smith, the famous huntsman of the Bramham Moor hounds, who has kindly added notes about hunting, and the management of a pack ; and to Mr. J. G. Elsey, the eminent steeple-chase trainer, who has given much valuable information about horses, and riding to hounds. The experience of such experts must ever carry great weight in forming conclusions. Differences of opinion must always exist, but success is ever the true touchstone of merit.

CONTENTS

A HUNTING CATECHISM

INTRODUCTION

THAT hunting has ever been the sport of kings, and the occupation of their leisure hours, there is ample evidence besides that of the immortal John Jorrocks ; and in connection therewith the tragic fate of King Edward the Martyr, who was so treacherously stabbed by the direction of his stepmother, Queen Elfrida (who wanted the Crown for her own son), while stopping on his way home from hunting to drink a cup of wine at her residence at Corfe Castle, and the accident to William Rufus in the New Forest will occur to every one.   English history further relates the fondness of the imperious Queen Elizabeth for the chase, and how she shot at stags driven past her in Windsor Forest ; while tradition yet lingers in the dales of Yorkshire that King James I., whose love of hunting became actually a passion, when staying at Nappa Hall in Wensleydale, had all the stags driven from the mountainous regions of Bishopdale and Langstrothdale Chase into Raydale, and made a " bag " of three hundred stags in one day.

Raydale is wonderfully adapted for such a slaughter, for in the midst lies Semmerwater, the first of the lakes, and one of the three natural ones (besides tiny tarns) that exist in Yorkshire, its companions being Malham Tarn in Craven and Hornsea Mere in Holderness. Semmerwater rejoices in a tradition of its own—how, on a wintry evening, a tired and belated wayfarer stopped at the prosperous village that then existed, and vainly asked for food and shelter at each cottage as he passed ; but, contrary to the rules of the very real Yorkshire hospitality that even yet exists in this wild district, the traveller was treated with scorn, and bidden to proceed on his way. When he had reached the last house he at length found one to befriend him, and in the morning he cursed that village, and, being an angel in disguise, sent to find out if certain rumours that had reached Heaven were true regarding the inhabitants of the place, his prayers were quickly heard, and a lake of considerable size rose up and submerged the village and its inhabitants. It is even averred that on a very still, calm day, when the lake is low and the water absolutely clear, the roof and chimneys of the houses may yet be seen, far down in the pellucid depths.

Beyond the south-western shore run two large valleys on either side, that terminate at length in a lofty mountain range, with a tongue of land between them, and guarded on their outer flanks by steep hillsides, along one of which—Wether Fell—the Roman road from Middleham to Ingleton winds its way. When once the stags had entered these valleys it must have been easy to hem them in with men guarding the lofty ridges, whilst as they rushed over the intervening tongue between the valleys, innumerable opportunities must have occurred of shooting them with the crossbow, and possibly with firearms which had lately come into use ; and also of driving the terrified animals with greyhounds into loosely-erected nets—which was a frequent method of taking stags in suitable localities.

Previous to this great capture of stags, Raydale had rung with the hunting horns when the ill-fated Queen Mary had been permitted to solace the weariness of her imprisonment in Bolton Castle hard by, where she was at first confined by Elizabeth, before being removed to Fotheringay Castle ; and she, as well as her son, King James, is said to have been the occasional guest of Sir Christopher Metcalfe at Nappa Hall, when intent on a hunting expedition.

Raydale the romantic is familiar also with the braying of other horns, for, from the days of the Normans, the curfew has been nightly wound at the village of Bainbridge, though no longer on the original trumpet, for Lord Bolton, rightly fearing that in these days of ubiquitous curio-seekers the ancient horn might find a resting-place in a suburban villa, or some equally unsuitable place, caused the venerable instrument to be placed in safety in the museum in Bolton Castle amongst other ancient relics of the dale, and substituted for it a replica, on which the curfew is now sounded.

An interesting account of the manner in which King Charles II. enjoyed fox-hunting, and testifying to the gallant manner in which he rode, is contained in a letter from my ancestor, Robert Fairfax, to his mother, dated from Wapping, December 6, 1687 :—

"MY DEAR MOTHER,—I had the honour on Thursday last to hunt with the King, which is a great diversion to me. The Duchess of Buckingham's gentlemen-at-arms lent me a horse. I wished many a time when I rode by him, that I might have had the privilege to have altered (*sic*) my mind to him. We hunted the fox, and the King rides very hard, as any one almost in the field. He got two falls, but received no harm. After hunting, the King and his nobles drink a cup of wine and eat a piece of bread under any old hedge, and after the King I assure you I had the honour to do the same out of his gilt cups. After that we go to the house where the King takes coach, and eat some hot soft beef, and burnt ale. The place is about five or six miles out of town."

Those who, by the accident of their lives, have been debarred from following the chase, whether such misfortune has occurred from want of opportunity, physical disability, or lack of inclination, can have no idea of the fierce instincts that are aroused, the excitement that is engendered, and the spirit of rivalry that is dominant, when hounds are racing with a breast-high scent, and one's whole being is imbued with but one idea—to be with them if one can. To experience this ecstasy of pleasure in its highest form it is necessary that all the conditions contributing thereto must be perfect. The fields must be of such size that the quarry, the hounds, and the horses have sufficient room to go at their best pace, for nothing is more prejudicial to a fast run than small enclosures. Among such the object of pursuit is continually afforded the opportunity of turning at each fence ; whereas, if the next one is not less than half a mile distant the fox, or hare, while it is still fresh will probably run down the middle of each field ; and as the hounds do not get checked by frequent fences, or have to unravel any twistings of the hunted animal, they are able to push along at a more continuous rate, thereby keeping closer to their prey, which consequently means a better scent, and therefore more speed.

Whyte-Melville never penned a truer sentence than when he wrote, " It is pace that puts life into the chase ! " Yet, essential as it is, there must also be present obstacles of a sufficiently formidable and varied character, to prevent the run from degenerating into an otherwise somewhat tame proceeding. This makes the whole difference between a gallop over the glorious pastures of the Shires, of the Tynedale in the North of England, or of the grand grazing-grounds of Meath and Galway in Ireland, and a fast run over the downs of the South of England or other open fenceless country. That this is generally recognised is shown by the prices willingly given for famous horses by those to whom money is no object, and who mean to be carried safely at the tail of the pack no matter how fast or far they run in the grass countries, when compared with the modest sum that should be sufficient to procure a perfect hunter in the land of downs and huge woodlands ; many provincial countries are chiefly remarkable for the amount of ploughed-fields that have to be crossed in a day's hunting, the smallness of the enclosures, and the steepness and roughness of their hills and valleys.

There is one thing, however, which binds all hunts in one brotherhood, in whatever kind of country their lot may be cast—one and all are dependent upon the hound for their sport. Without its marvellous gift of scent hunting would consist merely of coursing, and the amount of interest and enjoyment which can be obtained in watching the hounds make use of their powers in unravelling the mazy shifts of their game is just the same in a fast galloping country or the reverse. Indeed, in this respect the rougher countries rather have the advantage, for the pursued has there so many more opportunities of using its cunning that the hounds are correspondingly called upon to make increased efforts to cope with its wiles.

Times are changing fast, and the old order gives place to the new. Whether hunting will continue to hold its own when great estates are broken up into small holdings it is impossible to forecast, but it will be a bad day for the nation if the horn of the hunter ceases to be heard in the land. Apart from the immense amount of money put into circulation through the agency of hunting, and the vast amount of employment directly and indirectly attributable to it, there is a bringing together of different classes of society that can be effected in no other way ; and they get to know and respect each other's good qualities in a manner that can but be for the very best interests of the nation, though possibly prejudicial to the political agitator, who prefers to get his living by setting class against class, instead of by honest labour.

CHAPTER I

ETIQUETTE

BY this term is meant that unwritten law of custom which, from the primitive tribal savage to the most finished diplomat, governs every action that is taken in common with others, and in which every beginner must be initiated, to avoid mistakes that may heap ridicule upon himself, or possibly bring him into friction with his companions. Every trade, every profession, and every sport and game is governed by it, thus enabling a heterogeneous multitude to join in a common pursuit in perfect harmony, if only the unwritten rules are understood by all and carefully observed. It originates in the first place in that courtesy which is innate in " Nature's gentleman " as far as conduct is concerned, and on this is grafted such customs as may serve to assist the carrying out of a common object, or the designing of and wearing a suitable dress ; while the appropriate language to be employed is usually both well adapted to express what is meant, and at the same time a protection, since the using of wrong terms points out the novice, and grates on the ear of the initiated. As an

instance of the latter it would sound equally
strange to hear a person talk of the " seat " of a
fox or the " kennel " of a rabbit ! and yet both
mean the same thing, and if the two sporting
terms were reversed would sound quite correct.

Q. What are some of the correct terms for
hunting ?

A. A stag " harbours." A fox makes a
" kennel," or " lair " ; a " kennel " or " lair " is
above ground but an " earth " is *below*. A hare
has a " form."

A stag has a " tail." A buck has a " single."
A fox has a " brush." * A hound has a " stern."
A hare has a " scut."

A fox when seen should be " tally-ho'd." A
hare found sitting in its form is " so-ho'd."

A fox's head is a " mask."

A fox's foot is a " pad."

A fox " goes to ground."

A "vixen" fox has a "litter of cubs." A "doe "-
hare has " leverets." A red-deer " hind " has
" calves." A fallow-" doe " has "fawns."

When a fox leaves a covert he " breaks," or
" breaks away."

When a beast of chase makes its way to a far-
off refuge, it makes a " point."

If a fox or hare is turned aside from the "line"
it is following, it is " headed." A stag is
" blanched."

A stag has " horns." A buck has " antlers."

If a stag takes refuge in water he " soils."

---

* This was anciently called "a bush "; from the same
origin arises, no doubt, "a bushy tail." It was also known by
the quaint appellation, " A holy-water sprinkle." *See* John
Guillams, "A Display of Heraldrie," p. 176, published 1638.

The footprints of a stag are the "slot," of a buck "the view," of a fox the "track," or "pad-marks."

The track of a hare in fields is its "doubling"; on the road its "pricking."

A hunting-whip is usually termed a hunting-"crop."

When a huntsman sends his hounds into the first covert to seek a fox, it is termed "throwing-off."

When hounds suddenly lose possession of the scent in a run, it is a "check."

When the huntsman proceeds with the hounds over ground where he thinks the scent may be recovered or "hit off," he is "making a cast."

When a huntsman stops the hounds during a run, and hurries with them to a spot further on the fox's line so as to get nearer to it, and thus avoid traversing all the ground the fox has travelled over, he "lifts" the hounds.

When a fox is viewed away from a covert, either a "view-holloa" is given, or a prolonged shout of "Gone away!"

When a fox is either killed or run to ground a "Who-whoop!" is raised.

A "bulfinch" is a high, straggling old thorn fence, which it is only possible to get to the other side of by crashing through a thin, weak place, and which cannot be jumped over.

"Timber" means any wooden fence, as a gate, stile, or post-and-rail.

An "oxer" is a fence made up of a bulfinch that has had its tall growers cut half through, and then laid towards the field, while under the branches thus laid is usually a concealed ditch; on the further side of the fence is a post-and-rail.

It requires a bold, far-jumping horse to cover all in its stride.

When an Irishman speaks of a "ditch" he usually means a "bank"! And when he talks of a "double-ditch" (or "double," for short), he is indicating a bank, with a ditch on each side. A plain ditch he calls a "gripe."

"Holding-up" a fox in covert means surrounding the wood, and preventing him from leaving it by making a noise, or otherwise frightening him back when he endeavours to do so.

"Heading" a fox is getting in his way and turning him from his direct line.

A "sinking" fox is one whose powers are leaving him in a run, through fatigue.

A "beaten" fox is one quite tired out.

A fox "runs short" when he begins dodging about instead of continuing on in a straight direction.

"Chopping" a fox is when he is caught without having an opportunity of giving a run.

"Marking a fox to ground" is when the hounds show that they know he is within by trying to scratch the earth open, to get at him.

Hounds "draw" a covert when they spread themselves out to try and find a fox. They "wind" him when they detect the scent, before he has moved from his kennel.

A "babbling" hound is one that is always giving tongue whether there is a scent or not. A "mute" hound is one that runs on the scent, without giving tongue at all.

A "laggard" is a hound that is in no hurry to leave the covert and join the others when they go away after a fox.

A young hound "enters" when he learns to

recognise and pursue the scent of any particular quarry.

Puppies when they can run about are sent out "to walk" with kind friends, chiefly farmers, who rear them till they are old enough to be brought into the hunt kennels. Those that will be kept to join the pack are then selected, and the others are "drafted."

A "skirter" is a hound which will not pack with the rest when running, but keeps rather wide on one side, hoping to get a view of the fox.

"Rounding" young hounds is removing the superfluous lower portion of the ear-flap.

"Stopping" an earth means stopping the fox out *during the night.*

"Putting-to" means doing the same thing in *the early morning.*

There are many little courtesies that help much to good fellowship and are very generally observed by all accustomed to hunt, but which may not occur to a novice, and the breach of them is apt to be rather irritating if it is not known that ignorance is the cause of their being omitted. It is, for instance, very annoying after getting off one's horse to open a refractory gate, or by doing a little "carpentering" to make feasible an otherwise impracticable fence, to be left pirouetting on one foot whilst you frantically make efforts to put the other in the stirrup and mount your excited horse, as your followers pour through the way you have made plain before them, instead of waiting a second till you are in the saddle again, ready to speed once more after the flying pack. The man who thus confers a boon upon his comrades should have a kindly thought bestowed upon him, and no matter the urgency no one should move on until he has swung his right leg over the saddle once more.   It is apt to lead, too, to a forcible ejaculation, if in the hurry of the moment the rider in front omits to give a closing gate just that necessary shove, and it closes with a bang so close to your horse's head there is scarcely time to pull up to avoid running into it; or, even still worse, if it catches the animal on the shoulder, which might have been avoided by a little timely courtesy on the part of your predecessor, and would not have cost him five seconds' delay.

It is not doing to others what he would they should do to him for a man to ride a horse he knows will kick at other horses into a crowd that is standing waiting its turn at a gate or a gap, for if it is kept standing still such a steed is certain to indulge its whim, and maybe seriously damage another horse or its rider.   Such an ill-tempered animal can only be taken safely amongst others when all are moving along, and a stoppage for a time is more than likely to be attended with evil consequences.   The precaution of affixing a red ribbon to its tail should at least be taken, that all may be cautioned from approaching too near one adorned with the rogue's badge.

It should hardly be necessary to urge that any one seeing a rider fall, and requiring help, should immediately go to his assistance, however fast and exciting the run may be.   Common humanity alone demands this sacrifice of what is but pleasure after all.   Yet it sometimes happens that such duty towards one's neighbour is selfishly shirked, and one very sad ending to a very fine horseman and most popular comrade will occur to the minds of those who are now middle-aged. A happier sequel to an accident—which might easily have also had a fatal result—once came within the experience of the writer, and may be worth recounting :—

A fox had broken away from a small spinney, the field consequently getting all away together, and we were apparently in for a fast gallop, when the fox was suddenly seen returning right through the crowd of horses, so that every one had to pull up and retrace their steps, and those who were first now became last, as they walked back towards the covert. I was proceeding leisurely along, expecting the fox to be headed in every direction, and that the hounds would probably chop him in covert, when a sudden movement amongst the foremost horsemen gave warning that the fox had escaped his fate, and was again away, running for his life. Having this time got such a very bad start it seemed no use to hurry until there was a chance of nicking in. I therefore cantered quietly down to a rather high bank, with a wide ditch full of water on the taking-off side, over which the hard riders had just jumped, while those whose discretion was better than their nerves were scurrying away as fast as their steeds could gallop, to circumvent the obstacle. I was some way behind everybody, and thought I was quite alone, when just as I was going to send my horse at the leap I suddenly became aware that some one far away on my left was also going at the same fence. Long habit causes one always to observe in a casual way whether a horse gets safely over a fence, without actually thinking about it or watching it, and though my attention was concentrated on jumping the fence before me, I became conscious that the horse in the distance had come to grief with its rider, and both had disappeared into the ditch.

All thoughts of taking the leap naturally departed, until it was seen what the outcome of the accident was going to be, and when the horse alone came into view, struggling up the edge of the ditch, I turned at once and galloped up to the scene of the disaster. It was startling to find a young lady floating on the surface, with her face submerged, for up to then I had not noticed whether the rider was a lady or a gentleman. She made no movement, and springing off my horse, I jumped into the water, and endeavoured to lift her up, but her own weight was so added to by the saturated habit I could do no more than keep her half raised out of the water. A gossoon, however, came running up, having seen me gallop off to what he intuitively guessed was "grief," and therefore not to be missed on any account, and our united exertions soon sufficed to get our charge safely on to *terra firma*. The first thing was to loosen her collar. Then, to my intense relief, another lady galloped up, having also observed me hurry away from the direction the field was going, and her assistance was most valuable ; but we both became rather alarmed since the patient showed no signs of life, not even breathing, while only the very slightest pulse could be felt at all. A suggestion of whisky was at once acted upon, and some was poured into her mouth as she lay on her back ; and then had she been an Irish-" man," we should have indeed been scared, since the whisky just remained where it was poured, and no attempt whatever was made to swallow it.

We consulted together what we should do next, and then, acting upon my suggestion, we rolled the young lady carefully on to her side and back again, which had the desired result, for she gave a spasmodic gulp, swallowed the whisky to our intense relief, and sat up. When the sure sign that a lady has come to herself occurred, and a hand was lightly passed to the back of her head, we felt at ease, and soon she was able with our help to walk to a neighbouring mansion, whilst the gossoon followed leading the three horses.

The cause of all this was that the young lady had but just recovered from a serious illness, and really had no business to be out hunting again so soon, but who can keep an Irish girl in the house when there is a hunter in the stable ready to go, and hounds are meeting in the immediate neighbourhood !

When, therefore, she fell into the water, the shock caused her immediately to swoon, and it is open to doubt whether she would not have been drowned, if no assistance had been forthcoming, for being face downwards the first faint effort to breathe again would have filled the lungs with water, and what would have then occurred it is impossible to say.

Tragedy and comedy are proverbially nearly allied, and the comic incident was to come next. The family of five daughters from the mansion we were approaching had been at the meet, and following the hunt on cars, and as soon as we had safely arrived at the house the first natural suggestion was that a hot bath, and then a rest, would be the best restorative. A difficulty as to the fulfilment of this advice was—*there was no bath in the house!*   Finally, a maid-servant made the proposal, " An why wouldn't a peggy-tub do, your honour ? " And so a peggy-tub it had to be.

It often happens that those who reside at a long distance from the meet, and know the direction in which hounds will proceed, try to save themselves and their horses extra fatigue, and stop a few miles short of the actual place of meeting. There can be no harm in this, if done with discretion, but on no account must the side of the covert that is going to be the first drawn be selected as the halting-place ; any foxes within will probably be disturbed by the sound of voices and laughter, and taking the hint will make their exit before the advent of the hounds. No one should stop within a couple of fields of a covert ; and preferably a lane should be chosen to wait in. Some may select the nearest public-house, but this can scarcely be recommended as a habit to be adopted !

For the same reason—fear of disturbing foxes that will be wanted during the day—when riding to covert do not indulge in a short cut down the rides of a covert that will be drawn later on, but rather take the longer route and keep to the road; then if no fox is forthcoming when the covert is drawn, at least there can be no uneasy feeling on the part of the rider in a hurry, or too solicitous of saving every possible yard of distance, that the blank draw has been caused by any fault of his doing.

There are men who get themselves disliked from their custom of starting late for the meet, and then galloping to covert on a hack—though nowadays probably a motor-car is used instead — and carelessly passing very fresh horses, especially when a groom is riding one and leading another. When a horse in front is seen to be nervous, or fidgety from freshness, it is both unmannerly, and also causing considerable risk, to pass it without slackening speed; for, apart from the danger of being unseated, much discomfort must be caused to the rider in consequence of too great speed on the part of the passer-by.

Great attention should always be paid to the wishes and directions of the M.F.H., whose authority must be unquestioned if order is to rule. So long as he is upheld in his position by the members of the hunt, he is entitled to exact obedience from all who partake in the day's proceedings. No one, whatever his rank or position in the country, should act directly contrary to his arrangements to show sport, such as riding down the side of a covert which is purposely left open for the fox to break there.

On one occasion many years ago a person of high position chose to disregard this rule, and saunter down the side of a gorse covert, whence it was hoped the fox would go, and the following scene took place between the M.F.H. and the offender :—

As soon as it was seen whither X was going, the Master called out in very conciliatory tones, "Oh, X, I want the fox to get away there! do you mind going back, please?" But X took no notice of the appeal, and merely sauntered on. "X," then exclaimed the Master rather sharply, "please go back, or the fox will not break where we want him to." To this appeal the only notice taken by X was merely to tilt his hat a little further back on his head, and raise his chin a

little higher. " D——n it, X,'" was the next
peremptory mandate, " *will* you go back, or I'll
take the hounds home at once." This ultimatum
at last had the desired effect, but the want of
tact and courtesy that required a threat of using
the last resource permissible to an M.F.H. was
much to be reprehended, and was commented
on severely by the whole field. X, it was considered, instead of showing himself to be a great
man, had proved himself a foolish one.

Though the M.F.H. is for the time being a
commander-in-chief, he must ever remember
that it is only through courtesy that he rules,
and that his authority is but unquestioned so
long as he wields it with discretion. He should
remember also that he is expected to comport
himself as a gentleman, and that it is no longer
the fashion to make use of expletives that were
common enough half a century ago, both in the
hunting-field and on parade, but are now as
much out of date in the one place as on the
other.

Mr. J. G. Elsey—a particularly keen sportsman
—has kindly sent me a criticism, evolved from
his experience, which has a considerable bearing
on this question, and which is as follows :—

" I have noticed in some countries a gentleman
hunting his own hounds, and a top-sawyer at the
game, expect the field and his whips to know
equally as much as himself, even to knowing
what is passing in that clever gentleman-hunts-
man's own mind ! And if by bad luck, in many
cases through no fault of their own, some
unlucky wights should go a bit contrary to the
huntsman's wishes, he will give them such a
shouting-scolding, if, indeed, worse language is

not used, that the whole field go hunting in fear and trembling, more afraid of doing wrong than anything else. Their enjoyment, therefore, must be of a very poor nature, and they move more like a funeral procession than an assemblage of jolly good fellows all round. The M.F.H. forgets within five minutes that he has ever spoken, but not so the unfortunate sportsmen who have been unpleasantly shouted at and blown up. These go home very much damped in their ardour and love of the game, in some cases nursing animosity against the M.F.H.; whilst the latter, having thought no more about it, goes home in ignorance of their feelings, and of their having a grievance against him; and then proceeds to give fresh people the same dose on the other three hunting-days of the week."

These trenchant observations may well be laid to heart by such M.F.H. as are apt to forget what is due to others in the heat of the moment and the excitement of the chase.

The late Sir Charles Slingsby was a very silent, and particularly courteous man, and yet he kept the huge fields that frequently came out with him—such was his fame, that riders came from far and near to see if report really spoke truly of the sport that he showed, and I have counted as many as two hundred scarlet coats out on one day—in perfect order, and one gentle rebuke from him produced more effect than the shouting-scolding mentioned above often does. On one occasion when hunting at Ribston, the late Captain Leslie, who then rode very hard, had been rather trying in the way he kept jumping close to the hounds when they were puzzling out an indifferent scent, and at last he jumped a fence into the very middle of the pack which had just checked on the far side of the hedge, and— tumbled off! Sir Charles galloped up to the fence and looked over, and now, thought we, he will just "let him have it" for overriding the hounds, and we listened intently. "I'm——" began Sir Charles, "I'm very glad of it!" and that was all the rebuke the culprit got, but he never forgot it.

On another occasion a stranger was particularly annoying in the way he kept thrusting after the hounds, and at length Sir Charles could stand it no longer. Galloping up to him, he held out his horn and exclaimed, "Here, sir, you take the horn! We cannot *both* hunt the hounds!" upon which the abashed stranger slunk back amongst the field, and ceased to give any further trouble.

Though the M.F.H. expects obedience from his subscribers, who willingly acknowledge his sway if they have confidence in him, he should be very careful not to give them cause for grumbling and nursing a grievance. For instance, it was scarcely judicious on the part of a well-known M.F.H. to gratuitously inform his largest subscriber, possessed also of most important coverts, that when the hounds met at a certain place in a few days' time they would first draw a famous gorse-covert, some three miles in the direction in which the said subscriber would come, and therefore if he waited there he would be saved that distance ; and then when the day came, and the subscriber had informed privately various friends from his part of the country of the "tip" he had received, so that all waited there together—it was not, I say, a wise thing on the part of the M.F.H. to go and draw a pet covert some three miles in the other direction, chuckling to himself how cleverly he had hoodwinked a portion of his field and got rid of them, as he loved to do. It was scarcely surprising that a pretty sharp lesson was administered to him, in that he received notice by the next morning's post that the hitherto annual large subscription would in future be withdrawn; and that until further notice he would not be permitted to draw that subscriber's coverts again.

The same M.F.H. was scarcely well advised on another occasion when, having advertised during a frost that on the first day possible for hunting there would be a meet at the kennels at 11 a.m., he was found some miles away, by a sportsman going to the meet, hurrying with the pack to a far distant covert at the very time he should have been at the fixture. His predilection for hunting by himself, that had again obtained ascendancy over him, was scarcely calculated to soothe the tempers of those left in the lurch, and was a grave abuse of the privileges of his position as head of affairs in the hunting-field.

Once also, but in a different manner, he strained the cordial relations that should exist between the M.F.H. and the owner of a very important estate, for having run a fox to ground in a field drain into which two or three hounds had forced their way, he thereupon decided to have that drain opened, cost what it might—the cost of relaying it, of course, being left for the owner to pay. Men and spades were sent for, and the task of opening up the drain was begun, while those out hunting, wearying of the undertaking, gradually, and with much grumbling at the loss of their day, departed to their homes.

The M.F.H. was deaf to all expostulations, and
when darkness approached he left one of the
whippers-in to remain until the task was finished,
directing him to obtain lanterns and have refresh-
ment brought for the diggers, who continued
working through the night.   When at length
the end of the drain was reached, after digging
throughout two large fields, it was discovered
that the fox and hounds had never remained
in the drain at all, but had gone right through,
for the precaution had never been taken of
going to the further end, to see if there were
any indications of those imprisoned having
escaped from their confinement.   The ludicrous
part of it was that, when the pack arrived at the
kennels, it was found that one of the missing
hounds had already arrived there an hour or two
previously, while the others turned up next day.
The serious part was that the owner of the estate
took great umbrage at such high-handed proceedings, and it required a most humble apology to
prevent that estate also being closed against the
hunt.

It is very obvious from the above narratives
that tact and thoughtfulness are most essential
qualities for every M.F.H. to possess.

Between the interests of hunting men and
shooting men unfortunately discord arises at
times, frequently either through the incapacity
or animosity of a keeper, often the servant of
a syndicate who have hired the shooting, and
have otherwise no connection with, or interest
in, that part of the country.   There are many
keepers to whom the very idea of a fox is much
the same as if it impersonated the Tempter of
Eve ! and having been brought up probably

on an estate where foxes were not allowed to exist, and been told from childhood that " where there were foxes there *could* be no game," he has never had the opportunity of studying the habits of the animal, and has believed all he has been told. What would such a man think of five litters of cubs on one estate—at Kirby Hall—and yet there were plenty of pheasants and partridges, while hares were so numerous that my father used to restrict us as boys to twenty-five hares a day when partridge-shooting, when we used often to pick out only the big ones to shoot, to make a fine display on our return in the evening ! And yet my father did not hunt himself ! ! And what would he think of the litters reared in Suffolk itself on several estates, such as at Westacre, where three times over four hundred brace of partridges have been killed in a day in October within the last few years, while there have never been less than five litters of cubs, and generally more ; and on another estate, a few miles off excellent bags of partridges are also made, and yet there are lots of foxes ? Can the said keeper show the same results under *his* system of killing any foxes who come on to his beat ? Or, perhaps, he salves his conscience by *only* killing the old foxes, that sadly common trick which Mr. Velveteens is apt to think he has done so cleverly, nobody knows anything about it ! If he has but one litter of cubs on an estate that should show from three to five litters, does he imagine that the M.F.H. does not know what is going on ? And if only cubs and no old foxes are ever seen, does he think that escapes attention, and that he himself is not a marked man ?

Partridges and pheasants can be protected from foxes when sitting by various methods,* and be it remembered that foxes live on many other articles of diet besides game, though naturally they will not refuse it if it comes in their way.

In defence of keepers, however, it may be justly urged that they are not always free agents in the matter of foxes, and a friend of great experience emphasises this in the following letter, which should carry great weight when selecting the right horse to put the saddle on :—

" It would hardly be fair to lay all the blame for want of foxes upon keepers alone. It is natural for a keeper to kill foxes unless told not to by his master, and such instructions should be given pretty straight. It is nearly always the master who should be blamed, and not the servant. I know shooting people who have exactly the feeling about foxes that you attribute to keepers, and with such masters how can you expect the servant to show any mercy to what is, after all, his natural enemy ?

" In one way a fox is a good friend to lazy keepers ; any harm done by any other vermin is always put down to the fox.

" No doubt we have shown that it is possible to have partridges and foxes, but it can only be done by the master insisting on having both. Rats, stoats, &c., are often neglected, and the fox gets the blame ; at the same time one must admit that foxes do harm. In our case I think they make us take care there is not much else to interfere with the nests."

As the bags of partridges obtained on this estate are very large, it is undoubtedly proved

* *Vide* " Shooting Catechism," p. 151.

there that a clever keeper can show both partridges and foxes, when both master and servant
are determined to have both ; but if the master
is lukewarm in the matter, the keeper is scarcely
likely to be keen about preserving foxes.   When
the keeper presumes to go contrary to his orders,
and spends his time in limiting the number of
foxes, instead of looking after the other vermin
on the estate, the bags of partridges will often
be also limited, whether any foxes are allowed to
be there or not.

Shooting syndicates should take into consideration what the habits and feelings are of the
district which they propose honouring with
their presence, before they make their bargain ;
and if the sport of the country is hunting they
should be prepared to act accordingly, and not
selfishly destroy the amusement of their neigh-
bours.   If they are not willing to behave with
good-fellowship, let them go elsewhere amongst
others of their own tastes and ideas.   Their
absence will be more welcomed than deplored
by the members of a hunt.

With regard to costume it is advisable that
the novice should go to firms of repute and
be guided by their advice, without running into
extremes of any description.   It is well to take
into consideration the character of the country
in which hunting will be pursued, for in
some of the wilder hunts one of the first considerations must be adequate protection from
the rough weather that will be met with, and
in a very bleak country ample skirts to the
hunting-coat to protect the thighs are almost
an absolute necessity.   It is much to be
regretted that fashion has so long enforced

the wearing of a tall hat with a scarlet coat, so
ill-adapted for its purpose as a head-covering.
It is an absolute nuisance in a high wind, making
it impossible to keep the head erect, besides being
most difficult to keep on, and is most unsuitable
amongst the branches and twigs of trees and
hedges ; whilst the velvet hunting-cap—such an
ideal headgear—is at present restricted to the
M.F.H. and his staff. It was not always so, and
at the time the writer began hunting many of
the field used to wear hunting-caps, but when
the fatal accident occurred to Henry Marquis
of Waterford, the conclusion was jumped to that
it was in consequence of his wearing a cap at
the time ; and the hatters promptly seized the
opportunity of pushing a head-dress that must
be constantly damaged and continually require
renewing. If hunting-caps are dangerous, surely
even fashion would not require huntsmen and
whippers-in to wear them exclusively, and yet it
is seldom that a hunt-servant meets with a broken
neck.

Many men suffer much from cold feet when
hunting, and often this is caused by having their
breeches too tightly buttoned below the knee ; or
the tops, or feet, of the boots too closely fitting.
The circulation of the blood is then impeded, and
cold feet are the result. The tops of the boots
should be just loose enough to pull on without
using boot-hooks, but yet be tight enough to
prevent rain running down inside the boots.

It is a mistake to have sharp rowels to spurs,
and many a man gets kicked off by a fresh horse,
which has begun to frisk in play but, being
pricked unconsciously by the efforts of the rider
to keep his seat, starts kicking and bucking in

earnest. Spurs are very seldom required for use, and when they are very few riders can use them with effect. For all general purposes, for setting off a smart boot, and also for just a touch in the horse's ribs as a reminder to make an extra effort, spurs with blunt rowels or none at all are fully as effective, and much safer than sharp ones. The sluggish horse that requires the latter is no mount for the ordinary rider.

The last question, but certainly not the least, is the amount of subscription that should be considered sufficient to qualify for the "membership" of a hunt, and to wear the hunt button accordingly. This is a very difficult matter to regulate, for circumstances must vary much in almost every case, and the subscription that is fixed for one of the fashionable hunts in the Midlands would be ludicrous for a small provincial pack, where few of those hunting are rich men, and where the fields that usually follow the hounds comprise, probably, never more than some two-score followers. The old, well-established rule is a very good one for ordinary hunts, that a person should give what he can afford to his own hunt; and that each hunt should hospitably welcome the members of their neighbouring hunts—otherwise Paul is robbed to pay Peter. This worked well in former days, when those who hunted were residents in the district, and it still answers with a very large proportion of provincial packs; but in the case of the fashionable hunts, and those which have large manufacturing towns within their borders, whose inhabitants belong to no one pack, but hunt with all that meet within reach, some other plan has to be adopted, that aliens should not "get their fun for nothing," if miserly inclined. " Capping " has been tried with some packs, but it is not carried out with the thoroughness with which it is in Ireland, where it is universal. The English packs seem to make too high a charge, which it is an object with some persons to avoid by any possible device. Irish packs invariably have one uniform charge of 2s. 6d., which *every one* pays except tenant-farmers—whether a subscriber or not—and which is levied at the meet, or on the road to the first draw.

In some cases where there are many rich men in a hunt, and the committee is entirely composed of such, the case of poorer residents is apt to be overlooked when fixing the amount of hunt subscriptions. Twenty-five or thirty pounds seems nothing to a man who counts his income by many thousands per annum, but it is a very great source of anxiety to the younger brother, or professional man, who has only a few hundreds a year to reckon upon, and a family to provide for, and who may be a far better sportsman than his richer compeer. Many such have to forego little luxuries to be enabled to hunt at all : they travel third-class, make the threadbare old suit last another year, and economise in numbers of ways that the rich man would never dream of, who need not deny himself anything in order to find the wherewithal for his hunting. And yet both are expected to pay the same subscription, in order to be qualified to wear the hunt button ! It is the many small men, not a few rich men, who are the backbone of every hunt, and if hunting is to be but a rich man's sport, it will not survive the attacks of its enemies.

CHAPTER II

ACCESSORIES

Q. WHAT are the main requirements in planning a hunting-stable ?

A. 1. Boxes sufficiently roomy for a tired horse to move about, without being unnecessarily large.

2. Good drainage.

3. Ventilation without draughts.

4. Flooring that will not get slippery.

5. Windows so arranged that a glare of light is not constantly beating down on the eyes of the inmates.

6. Walls that do not reflect light.

7. Well-arranged manger and hay-rack.

8. Some method for having water continuously available for a horse to drink.

9. Arrangements for fixed artificial light.

10. If there is no stall in the stable, some plan for pillar-reins.

11. If expense need not be considered, a washing-room apart from the stables is a welcome addition to the comfort of the men, and saves labour.

12. A convenient hay-loft, place for straw, and granary.

13. A convenient place for storing carrots, &c.

14. A conveniently arranged saddle-room.

15. An ample supply of fresh water.

16. An ample supply of hot water.

17. Bedrooms for the men, and, if possible, a mess-room for them.

18. Arrangement for drying wet clothing, airing saddles, &c.

19. Detached boxes for sick horses.

20. Where practicable, a riding-school, or covered-in place where young horses can have their first lessons in breaking, &c.

21. A small paddock for turning out a sick horse ; and, if possible, some larger paddocks for turning out horses in summer, or when thrown out of work for any reason.

22. An airy situation, without damp.

Q. How large should a box be for ordinary use ?

A. A tired horse does not need a large box, for what he requires is merely sufficient room to alter his position from time to time to ease stiffened limbs, and to lie down and roll. If the horse after a hard day's work is tied up, he can only relieve himself by flexing first one leg and then another, all his weight being continually thrown on to the other feet. It must be remembered that a horse's foot is outwardly composed of a horny box, which is practically inelastic, and if his weight is imposed upon a foot for some time, the circulation in the inner parts is apt to become congested, especially at a time when the whole of the system is debilitated by a hard day's work. This congestion may be the parent of many evils, and to obviate it a horse should always be put into a box, and not a stall when thoroughly tired. In a box, however small, a horse is continually moving about, and as he does so keeps relieving the pressure on each foot in turn ; and he also is much more predisposed to lie down, thus taking his weight off his limbs, and to rest.

An idle horse or a sick horse, however, needs more room, and should have a larger box, as it is his only opportunity of taking exercise. A horse when free is continually moving about, for the greater portion of the twenty-four hours, resting but for short periods, and therefore, when confined in a stable, and not being exercised, he requires a good roomy box in which he can work off superabundant energy. In such boxes, however, much more straw will be used up than in smaller ones, and thus the horsekeeper will find his expenses somewhat increased.

For a box for horses in hard work, a width of 9 feet is sufficient by 14 feet long ; this particular width is convenient in other ways, as it is just the length of an ordinary railway-sleeper. A box is not necessarily always set apart for the use of horses. It may, for instance, be temporarily required for a cow, or even a litter of little pigs ! It is well to use foresight, and think what might be some day required, and a cow would soon get a bad pair of knees if she was tied up in a box with a hard floor. (Some persons may not be familiar with the fact that when a cow rises from lying down she raises her hind-quarters first, putting all her weight on to her knees, and then with a sudden effort springs up on to her fore-feet. A horse does exactly the contrary, raising itself on its fore-feet first, and then rising on to its hind limbs.)

It is easy then, with a width of 9 feet for a box, to make a temporary platform of sleepers for a cow to rest on, which can be removed when the box again returns to its primary use for a horse. Sleepers are, however, never carefully cut to size, and therefore those should be selected that would be available for use when required.

For a sick box, or for an idle horse, a box may be 12 feet by 14 feet; even 14 feet square will not be too large, if the expense for extra litter is no object. Boxes for stallions are frequently 18 feet square.

Q. What system of drainage can be recommended?

A. Perhaps the best of all is some form of surface drainage that can be easily cleansed, and does not sink into and saturate the flooring.

Q. How can this be carried out?

A. Either by using red or blue, specially prepared, channelled bricks, which must be laid to have a slight fall; or by having a concrete bed, with cobble stones above, imbedded in a layer of cement, and then grouted.

Q. What thickness should the concrete and cement be respectively?

A. The concrete, which should be mainly formed of rough broken bricks or something similar, should be about a foot thick, and the cement above about 9 inches, the proper fall being now attended to. The cobbles should be imbedded about half their depth when the cement is in a fairly stiff state; and the work is more easily performed, if only a narrow breadth is done at a time, so that a man can easily reach to fix the stones in their places in the soft cement.

As soon as one breadth is finished the next should
be begun. When all are set, and the cement has
sufficiently hardened, a little liquid grouting can
be added to obtain the requisite level between
the stones. These latter should not be set too
closely together, to afford facility for sweeping
away any accumulation that may lodge between
them. Such a floor never gets slippery, and
always affords good foothold when horses are
rising up or lying down. There should be an
opening through the bottom of the wall, with
a channel leading to it from the stall or box, to
conduct all liquids to the outside, where some
arrangement must be made for their removal,
either by drains or otherwise.

Q. If underground drains are used in the
stable instead of surface ones, what are important
points to attend to ?

A. In the first place the surface may be kept
flatter, which is a decided advantage, for the
necessary slope can be adjusted in the underground drain, and there is therefore less strain
on a horse's limbs than when he is constantly
standing on an inclined plane.

There should be as few angles as possible, for
these are apt to arrest any solid particles that
may find their way into the drain, and wherever
one is absolutely necessary it should be made as
obtuse as the ground permits.

There should be some simple trap at the
inflow ; and the whole length of the drain should
be easily accessible, and capable of being
thoroughly cleansed every day.

Q. Is not "ventilation" and a "draught"
often the same thing ?

A. Unfortunately, such is the case. Frequently ventilation that is designed for use in the hottest days of summer is made use of in the depths of winter, and it should be thoroughly impressed on all grooms that no animal can thrive in a draught ; while the better groomed a horse is the more sensitive does his skin become, and the more likely is he to catch cold. An old Spanish proverb says, " Death comes in with the wind through a hole," and there is a great deal of truth in this. Fresh air is most beneficial, but even more so is the avoidance of a draught, and where this is not attended to, constant colds are the inevitable penalty. Ventilation should be independent of windows. Where it is practicable it is a good plan to have a small opening through the wall near the surface of the ground, if there are nothing but boxes ; but if there are stalls the ingress of the air must be at a higher level. There should be a corresponding outlet passing through the roof, guarded by louvre boards, which should be placed over the passage, clear of the boxes, so that if a sudden down draught should commence before it is detected it will not come direct upon the horses. A sliding board should be fixed to each so that the openings can be arranged to a nicety in a second, or, if necessary, be closed altogether. A down draught should never be permitted to continue, but must be stopped at once as soon as detected. A horse racked up, with a draught playing upon him which he cannot escape by moving his position, is an unfortunate object but too often seen. Ventilation directly over a horse's head is very efficient in the dog-days, but very dangerous in the winter months.

Q. Are the eyes of horses affected by a strong light ?

A. It is, perhaps, not so much a strong light that is pernicious as light reflected from certain spots, from which there is no escape. Such are windows placed in front of a horse that is constantly tied up—as in a stall ; or light spark-ling from glazed bricks, especially white ones, with which the inner surface of walls are often adorned, to give a smart, clean appearance. Glazed bricks can do no harm in the passages, but should never be used in either boxes or stalls.

Q. Then what material should be used in their place ?

A. There is nothing cleaner or more whole-some than black varnish, which need not be carried higher up the wall than the height of a horse, if a little variation is preferred ; and above that some light tint of " Duresco."

Q. Where can black varnish be obtained ?

A. At any colourman. If preferred, it can easily be made at home from the following ingredients :—

Black Varnish for Stables.

Tar	...	...	...	...	2 gallons.
Lime	...	...	...	...	3 lbs.
Turpentine	...	...	...	...	1 pint.

Boil the tar, and then add the lime and turpen-tine. Put the mixture on hot. The more turpentine is added the quicker the varnish will dry.

If the varnish should stick to the hands, or touch the coat of a horse, or anything similar, it can be removed by using soft soap and a very little turpentine.

Q. What should always be attended to, if the sides of the walls are left rough, as built ?

A. That no excrescences or inequalities exist in the bricks, as a very slight ledge may cause the hoofs to hitch when a horse is rolling, and a fatal accident may result. If there is any panelling employed either for partitions or otherwise, every board should be placed perpendicularly, and not horizontally, for it is extraordinary how little power a horse possesses of releasing itself when lying on its back, and what a very tiny space between two boards may effectually cause it to get " cast," if the hoofs get caught in it. Fatal injuries may ensue from the struggles of the captive to release itself.

Q. What is a good arrangement for mangers and hay-racks ?

A. Mangers are now frequently made of iron, which gives the advantage of being easily kept clean ; but the drawback is that such are necessarily small, and consequently an excitable horse, which constantly raises its head while eating, every time drops some of the oats among the bedding. Many horses do this on purpose, and afterwards scrape away the straw, when such is used for litter, and pick up the scattered grain ; but if other material is used for bedding, peatmoss, sawdust, or shavings, the oats cannot always be recovered. Iron mangers should always have a " lip " round the inside to prevent a common trick amongst horses of shoving some of their oats out with their muzzle when a manger is small ; and to stop this practice, when the mangers are wooden ones, they should always be of considerable length, so that an animal can spread the feed along it, without shoving it out altogether.

A manger should, of course, be low, but unless boarded down to the floor, it should not be low enough for a horse to knock its knees against the bottom of it when feeding, a trick that some adopt, and often the cause of a very troublesome " big " knee. One advantage iron mangers possess is that horses are much less prone to catch hold of them when being " dressed," which sometimes ends in contracting the vice of " windsucking," or " crib-biting."

Hay-racks should always be as low as the manger, for overhead racks offer great facility for the intrusion of hay-seeds into the eyes, when the head is raised to pull out the hay.

It is preferable to have water always present, so that a drink can be obtained whenever an animal is thirsty, and many mangers are now on the market having a hay-rack and chamber for water attached, all being in one piece. Where such has not been fitted, often a corner of the box can be utilised, and a low brick place erected to hold a zinc pail of water. This should be built in the form of a sugar-loaf, broad at the base, and contracting to almost the width of the bucket at the top, with a hollow to hold the vessel.

The object of having this form is to prevent a horse from standing close to it when drinking, so that, if he is irritated by flies and suddenly jerks a knee up, there will be room to do so without touching the bricks.

The bucket should be lifted out, emptied, and refilled at stated hours, to ensure the water being always fresh and sweet. It is an undoubted fact that most horses imbibe less fluid during each twenty-four hours if water is always within reach, than when it is offered in the usual way.

Q. Do not horses prefer pond water to drink to spring water ?

A. Undoubtedly they do, but care should be taken that no impurities either from a manure heap, house drain, or otherwise, trickle into it, for horses are very subject to a kind of typhoid fever, if they are supplied with impure water. When the water supply comes from a well, no surface water should be admitted, or rainfall from a roof, especially if the latter is of thatch. Water from a roof after a prolonged drought is ever to be looked upon with suspicion, for an accumulation of droppings of birds and other contaminations get swept into the reservoir, and illness, apparently obscure, frequently results.

Whenever there is any doubt about the purity of water, and no other supply can be obtained, it is a wise precaution to boil what is offered to the animals to drink.

Where no gas or electric light is available, there should always be strong nails fixed in convenient places, on which to hang the lanterns that must be used while the men are at work ; too much precaution cannot be taken to guard against the awful visitation of a fire in a fully-occupied stable.

If such should unfortunately occur, horses should never be turned loose to find their own way out, but each horse must be taken out separately, or one horse may block the exit altogether. It is well to remember that a horse can often be ridden out, which is too terrified to

allow itself to be led out; and also that, if a horse
utterly refuses to move, it may be induced to do
so by throwing a rug over its head, and thus
deadening the senses of sight, smell, and hearing.

Obstinate horses should be left to the last, or
willing horses may have to be sacrificed in the
end, which could have been safely removed
during the time spent in struggling with the
panic-stricken one.

Where gas or electric light is used, care must
be taken that no horse can gain access to it at
any time, or some accident will occur. A gas-
bracket with a movable arm can often be hidden
away in a recess in the wall, and the opening
secured so that an animal cannot possibly tamper
with it.

Q. Why are pillar-reins necessary in a stable?
A. Besides the convenience of fastening a
horse to them that is ready for mounting, without his being able to rub the bridle as he would
do if fastened to the manger, they are very useful
for other purposes. It often improves the mouth
of a young horse which unfortunately is harder
on one side than the other, or who bores at the
bit, to be placed on the pillar-reins for an hour or
so each day, and allowed to stand there champing
and playing with his bit, which he will learn to do,
instead of maintaining the same dull, heavy pull
that he is inclined to when ridden. Sometimes
also a " crib-biter," " wind-sucker," or " weaver "
can be thus fastened up with advantage before
going to work, when he would otherwise indulge
in his evil propensity to his detriment, if racked
up in the usual way.

Q. If a washing-room is erected, where should it be placed?

A. At the back of the saddle-room fire, so that hot water can be conveniently drawn from its boiler. It is a great convenience, when horses come in from work, to have a covered-in place where their feet can be washed out and attended to, before going into their stable. Such a room is constantly in requisition for many purposes.

Q. Is a glass case for clean steel articles such as stirrups, curb chains, &c., necessary besides the usual fittings of a saddle-room, such as brackets for saddles, pegs for bridles, a saddle-horse for cleaning saddles, and a large quadruple hook from the ceiling for cleaning bridles?

A. It is very useful indeed, as a glance shows whether any article requires attention. It is better not to put such a case over the chimney-piece, the usual place selected for it, as steam from a boiling kettle or pan may find its way into it (though such an occurrence is generally found to be absent in actual practice). The process of " Sherrardizing " steel, invented by Mr. Cowper-Coles, has, however, quite done away with the fear of rust, and has, in consequence, largely reduced labour in the saddle-room. All bits, stirrup-irons, chains, &c., submitted to this treatment (which is very cheap), only require washing clean on return from work, and then a rub with a chamois leather sends them forth again as bright as silver, without requiring polishing with the steel-burnisher as usual.

Q. What are the actual necessaries for one horse?

A. 1 leather head-collar.

2 leather head-collar reins, with chain ends and logs (the chains should, if possible, work behind boarding, so that there is no chance of their getting entangled in the horse's fore-legs ; and this is the more necessary when only one rein and log is used). At the junction of the leather and chain there should be a ring sufficiently large not to pass through the ring on the manger through which the chain passes. The weight of the log then generally rests on the ring of the rein, and is not always dragging at the horse's head. In a box these head-collar reins are not required.

1 rack-chain with spring-hook.

1 pair leather pillar-reins, with brass spring-hooks.

1 hempen halter.

1 watering snaffle.

1 double-rein snaffle (with thick mouthpiece) and noseband.

1 martingale.

1 Cheshire martingale.

1 double-rein bridle.

1 saddle, with broad girths (Melton) and three-bar stirrups (with Prussian side-irons) and leathers.

1 exercising saddle complete.

2 suits Witney blanket horse-rug, to buckle at chest.

2 rollers.

N.B.—If the rugs are so made as to buckle round the chest and under the girth (which is strongly recommended), the rollers are not required.

2 striped night-rugs, to buckle at chest.

2 sets woollen bandages.
1 set linen bandages.
1 pair knee-caps.
1 stable shovel.
1 stable fork.
1 stable lantern.
1 horse-pick.
1 mane-comb.
1 curry-comb.
1 steel burnisher.
1 dandy-brush.
1 horse-body-brush.
1 water-brush.
1 bit-brush.
2 stable pails.
1 cane basket.
1 corn measure.
1 sieve.
Chamois leather.
1 set dusters.
2 sponges.
1 singeing lamp (gas), with 12 feet tubing.
1 clipping-knife.
1 stable-broom.
1 oat-bin with lock, with division in middle.

Q. What other articles should be at hand in a hunting-stable ?

A. An oat-crusher and a hay-chopper should always be there, for use for horses that do not masticate their food properly. A dumb jockey is needed if young horses are bought, and require breaking ; and a pair of web lunging-reins are often required for exercising fresh horses, or teaching young ones to bend to the bit. In addition, a hair rope is very useful if a horse has to be tied up to be cast, for it does not chafe the skin like a hempen one.

Q. What are the chief requisites in a saddle ?
A. That it should be roomy enough to be comfortable to sit in, and to distribute the rider's weight equally on the horse's back. Too small a saddle is both uncomfortable, and even danger- ous, for many a rider has suffered permanent ill- health from coming down on the pommel or cantle of the saddle, which has, indeed, been on occasion actually fatal. A saddle ought not only to be well stuffed, but constant care is required to prevent the stuffing working into hard lumps, which are sure causes of sore backs ; it needs careful drying after use, and beating with a light cane to keep it right.

The tree must be very carefully fitted, especi- ally when a horse does not possess naturally " a saddle back," but is either low, or rounded, in the withers, or, perhaps, has a hollow back. Some horses that are otherwise well shaped have such high thin withers that the tree of the pommel is very liable to press upon them there ; and whenever a sore place occurs either on the withers, or on the spine under the cantle, it is always particularly difficult to cure. From there being no flesh over the bone in either place a bruise is a serious matter. It is always advisable when first mounting to try if at least the forefinger can easily pass under the pommel in front, and the cantle behind, and if it cannot do so there is not sufficient room. The remedy for the moment is to obtain a thick felt numnah, or a piece of old rug to place under the saddle. A linen rubber will do, if very carefully folded smooth, but there is a danger of its becoming wrinkled, which would itself cause a sore. Some horses have such well-formed backs that a saddle would almost stay in its place without girths, but others can never prevent their saddles from moving. The best means of preventing this, especially with ladies' saddles, is to have the sides of the tree prolonged far down the shoulder, which gives a better grip to the saddle.

A very important point is to see that the pommel does not pinch the withers. It is better that it should be too wide, which can be remedied, than too narrow, though both are faults.

Q. Are leather-lined saddles to be recommended?

A. They suit some horses very well, especially half-bred ones. The leather requires to be constantly oiled, to keep it soft. Some thoroughbred horses have such very tender skins that leather lining does not seem to answer with them.

Q. Is indiarubber-sponge lining good?

A. It is excellent, and if attended to when in use, and washed from time to time in the summer, will last a long time. Such saddles should be kept in the dark, as in a cupboard, and a small saucer of turpentine placed near in a saucer, the fumes of which help to preserve indiarubber.

Q. Are ventilated saddles really efficient?

A. They can be praised for keeping the backs cool; and the one invented by Robson of York is very highly spoken of indeed by many ladies who hunt in it. It is fitted with air chambers between the seat and the stuffing. It is claimed that they are lighter than ordinary side-saddles.

Q. What are the chief improvements in side-saddles ?

A. Doing away with the off-side crutch has largely increased the safety of ladies in a fall when hunting ; but it had its advantages in other ways, which are now absent. Ladies often found it a relief to place some of their weight on it by resting their hand there when tired ; and by this action the balance of the body was kept more in the centre of the saddle, whereas now a tired lady is apt to throw most of her weight on the pommels and the stirrup, and so drags the saddle on to the near side. The consequence of this is a wrung wither on the opposite side, which has undue pressure thrown upon it.

Another advantage that has been lost is that an extra screw-hole on the off-side enabled the third pommel to be quickly changed, so that the rider could continue her homeward journey on the reverse side to the ordinary way, a great relief both to herself and the horse. Perhaps in these days of apron-skirts this method might have disadvantages of its own it did not formerly possess !

Q. Is it not a wise precaution for ladies to use safety-stirrups ?

A. Most certainly ; no precaution of this kind should be omitted whereby the danger attendant on a fall may be minimised. It is a great advance in this direction that the old round skirt, so often the cause of a lady being " hung up," and meeting with a serious accident in consequence, has been replaced by the modern aprons.

The very broad crutch for the left knee that has recently been introduced is also a step in the right direction, and is most favourably reported on for ease and comfort by ladies who are now using it.

Q. Are raw-hide girths as good as ordinary ones ?

A. Except for fashion they are better, for they keep a horse very cool, and take such a good grip they need not be drawn so tight as the others. If they are kept well oiled they seldom gall a horse, and many very thin-skinned thoroughbreds can be ridden in these girths, whom the ordinary ones would rub quite raw.

Q. If an ordinary girth does gall a horse, more especially a young one that is still low in its withers and carries its saddle too forward, what is a useful remedy ?

A. A piece of soft string—there is nothing better than an old silk shoe-lace—should be tied round the webbing sufficiently tight to bend the edge outwards that is doing the mischief. There is then nothing to do harm, and as the withers grow up the saddle will get further back, and the evil will cure itself.

Q. What is a good preservative for saddles and bridles ?

A. Common yellow bar-soap—the same that is used for washing floors—is better than any saddle paste, for it keeps the leather soft, and never stains hunting breeches on a wet day. Unlike most pastes too, which often make a saddle as slippery as ice, and difficult to sit in if a fresh horse jumps about, leather treated with yellow soap gives a good grip (unless it gets covered with white dust from the paste used for cleaning white breeches, which can make any saddle almost unrideable for the time being).

The writer has himself used nothing but bar-soap for forty years, and it was in use in his father's stables for many years previously, so he has ample experience of its qualities.

Q. What kind of numnahs can be recommended ?

A. Numnahs often play an important part in stable economy, for where there are several horses the same saddles often have to serve for different animals. Felt numnahs are apt to shrink when a horse sweats freely, but something of this kind is much wanted. The writer some years ago obtained some white numnahs both for a lady's and a gentleman's saddle from Mr. Morris, a saddler at Cirencester, and can give unstinted praise to them, but he has never seen them elsewhere. A leather numnah is often useful towards the end of the season, if a back is becoming frayed and tender, but it must be well oiled when used in such a case.

Q. If a horse hits its fetlocks, as some do when tired, or in deep ground, is there any especially useful boot to obviate the evil ?

A. An excellent one for this purpose is made of leather in two parts, each shaped to the joint but only extending about a third of the way. The pieces are joined together at the top by a strap that buckles, and goes all the way round the limb. When the boot is struck by the

opposite foot it either does not move at all, or
else turns round so that the other part takes its
place, while being so loose mud does not stay
inside, if it gets in, and make a sore place.

For long-striding young horses, and those that
are apt to strike their back-sinews with their
hind hoofs, a serge boot, brought out by the
writer about thirty-seven years ago, has proved
most useful. It consists of two thicknesses of
serge, or cloth sewn together in large " diamonds,"
to go easily round the leg, and fasten with four
or five small straps. The advantage of this
fastening is that the bandage can be put on quite
loose, and is still safe. A mare of the writer's
won at Punchestown in 1879, and wore an
especial pair of black cloth bandages of this
description, because when racing she was in the
habit of going through the walls, and it was
feared she might do so on this occasion.
Kittiwake was ridden by the late Captain Morris,
7th Hussars, who said afterwards how fortunate
it was her legs had been thus protected, for she
went right through the wall and cut through the
two top straps. If she had been bandaged in the
ordinary way, and the strings had been thus cut,
the trailing bandage would in all probability
have become entangled round her legs, and
brought her to grief, or compelled her rider to
pull up to take them off.

CHAPTER III

HUNTING

THE motives inducing people to hunt are very various, but when once the object of pursuit is found and on foot, whether it is a stag, fox, or hare, one spirit dominates every one for the time being, trouble and cares are for the moment flung to the winds, and everything is forgotten in the excitement of the chase.

It is surprising to witness the celerity with which the different units that compose the field group themselves under different leaders, as soon as the covert is left behind, into divisions which are well defined to the close observer, and each of which, unless hopelessly thrown out or tailed off, lays the flattering unction to its soul that it has seen the run thoroughly from start to finish. It is not, indeed, necessary to jump every fence the hounds cross to be really in the run ; and even those gallant riders who care for nothing except being at the very tail of the pack, and whose ardent wish it is to be the first over every big fence, do not always see the incidents of the chase so well as those who have never jumped a fence at all, if lanes and gates have fortunately proved

5

convenient. It is not given to every one to be blessed with the necessary nerves to enjoy jumping big fences, and though the acme of pleasure can scarcely be felt at the conclusion of a gallop unless there is within the rider's breast an exultant glow of satisfaction at having gone well, and that the good horse under him has carried him gallantly over formidable fences, still there is a very large sense of triumph to be enjoyed by those who have contrived to see the whole run, even though they avoided those places the leaping of which has given the other so much satisfaction.

The rider who can hold his own with the best, and yet has a perfect knowledge of hounds' work, is a lucky man indeed, for he is a sportsman of the highest class. Such a one, although he may enjoy to the full the big fences, will never ask his horse to take one unless there is a necessity for so doing, and willingly acknowledges that the position he may hold in a run depends far more upon the sagacity and cleverness of the generous animal he may ride than upon his own prowess, though some riders appear to think that the whole credit belongs to them alone! But the man who thoroughly understands hunting has had an additional pleasure the whole time in noting how the hounds have done their part, even when the pace has been so great that it has taken him all his time to keep near the pack, which he probably could not have accomplished had he been less imbued with the natures of both the pursued and the pursuer; whilst in a slow hunting run he derives much satisfaction in watching each turn in the game, when the man who hunts only to ride in front feels but dissatisfied and bored at the slowness of the pace.

It is well to visit other packs from time to time, and see how things are conducted there, and the methods of different huntsmen, for new ideas are thus gained, and probably old ones may be discarded. It is easy to persevere in a fault for a long time, without discovering that one is in a wrong groove, until something occurs to open one's eyes; and this is more likely to occur through moving about than by staying at home, for life is not long enough for any one person to acquire everything there is to be learned about any pursuit, and it takes a long time to acquire fresh truths through personal observation alone. But man is fortunately able to communicate his ideas, so by travelling about and meeting fresh experts a stock of knowledge may be gained that would otherwise have remained more or less a sealed book to the solitary inquirer.

Though the main outlines of hunting must ever remain the same, methods of carrying them out must vary according to the nature of the country, for what can be more different than the pastures of high Leicestershire and the flints, and arable, and big woods of Hampshire! and while a rapid cast is absolutely necessary to get away from the huge crowd in the one place, it would be fatal in the other where the cold-scenting nature of the soil requires hounds to be left alone to puzzle out the line for themselves. Each of these countries, again, differs from the wild moorland regions, which so many packs in the north and west of Britain possess for happy hunting grounds, and which, indeed, mostly show excellent sport to their devoted followers. Strangers out for the first time do not always feel comfortable when asked to gallop over rough ground, with rocks and holes everywhere concealed in the thick heather, and yet often those whose hunting is confined to such districts, and to whom use has become second nature, feel just as uncomfortable when a fox takes them down into the vale below and they are required to jump unwelcome fences !

There is one boon so great that its value cannot be estimated, not only to the nation at large, but also to every hunt—the fearful scourge of rabies has no longer to be feared, thanks to the courage and determination of Mr. Long in stamping it out once and for all—the most valuable piece of real statesmanship that has been done in this generation. The memory of this achievement will ever remain a monument to his wisdom in persevering to its attainment against the opposition of an interested faction, who grumbled at the uncontrolled freedom of their pet-dogs being interfered with. There is no longer this danger to be dreaded, when puppies are out at walk, or hounds left out when hunting, and in a few years the ravages of this terrible disease will possibly be forgotten. Yet in several instances whole packs of hounds were destroyed through this cause.

Within the writer's recollection in the autumn of 1867 the Bedale hounds returned one evening from hunting, and about seven o'clock a wet and draggled hound turned up at the kennel, which the feeder admitted, thinking it was one of the young hounds that had been out that day, one or two of whom had not come home with the pack. He fetched a light, and stooped down to look more closely at it, when it sprang at him and bit him through the chin. Fortunately for the welfare of the pack, the precaution had been taken of tying the hound up by himself on arrival, and therefore, as far as my memory serves me, no other hounds were bitten, for this one shortly afterwards went raving mad and had to be destroyed. The man bitten underwent a course of treatment, and it was confidently hoped he had escaped all ill consequences; and when I arrived home on leave from my regiment early in the following February, I anxiously asked how the patient was, and was informed he seemed perfectly right. This was on a Wednesday, and as fate would have it the poor fellow was taken ill that very night, and died at the end of that week.

Rabies was very prevalent just then, and shortly after the occurrence at the Bedale kennels, my father's keepers were going out rabbiting at Thorpe Green, having with them several terriers belonging to me. According to the report I afterwards received, just as they started a strange dog appeared on the scene, and attached itself to them, whereupon one of the men suggested they should allow it to come on, to see if it was any good. It immediately, however, began fighting and quarrelling with the other dogs, and it was not till it had been well thrashed with sticks and battered with spades that it at length withdrew. All the dogs out were at once fastened up and examined, and only those allowed to go about that showed no signs of scratches at all, while those who showed any tears in their skin, however slight, were kept chained up and carefully secluded. It was well this precaution was taken, for all those fastened up died from rabies, excepting one, who had a slight scratch that might have been done by a thorn, while one of the keepers said he was absolutely certain this one had never been in the fray at all. Still he was kept isolated for about six weeks, and as he was a dear old dog, and a great favourite with every one, a very anxious time was passed until he was pronounced free from the infection. Those who have had experience of this dreadful disease are, indeed, grateful to Mr. Long, and are truly thankful there is now no risk of incurring its ravages.

A huntsman needs to be a bold rider, for he is often required to jump a big fence, when making a cast, while the rest of the field are standing still and merely looking on, and he must be always sufficiently close to his hounds in a run to see what is taking place, and to afford them assistance if they require it ; at the same time he must be a careful rider or he will get to the end of his horse's powers before the end of a really fine chase. It is absolutely necessary that both he and his whips should be well mounted, for otherwise they cannot do the work expected of them, nor is it right that their lives and limbs should be placed in jeopardy through niggardliness in purchasing their horses. At the same time it is not necessary they should be mounted on unblemished animals fit to take prizes at a show, and many a sound, good hunter may be picked up cheaply that will carry a hunt servant to perfection, whose drop in price is due only to some accident that mars its looks in the eyes of the ordinary purchaser.

There is much in a day's hunting, besides

the pleasure of riding a good horse, that helps to constitute the glamour thrown over its followers by the chase, and the various phases almost resemble different chapters in a novel. To those who understand the game, who are capable of reading as they run, every incident brings with it its own special interest and charm. The mode of drawing, the knowledge the huntsman displays of the likely haunts of his quarry, the style in which the hounds search different nooks and corners, the way in which advantage is taken of each varying current of wind, are all subjects of interest to the keen enthusiast, who makes a mental note of all he sees ; and when the game is on foot, even while it still clings to the shelter of the covert, hesitating to seek safety in flight, there is much to be learned from the cunning of the hunted animal and the sagacity of its pursuers.

One of the chief dangers to hunting has only arisen within a comparatively few years—the too frequent use of barbed wire, which, when concealed in a fence, is a veritable death-trap. Even with excellent arrangements for its withdrawal during the hunting season, and the most cordial co-operation of the farmers, it is inevitable that some strands are overlooked which have been used to strengthen a weak place in a hedge, and which are the most dangerous of all, for they are the least suspected. On a large estate timber for making up gaps is usually supplied gratis to the tenants, a boon which in former days was freely made use of ; but small freeholds are without this source of supply. Prizes at local shows for produce of farms where *no barbed wire* is in use, help considerably to mitigate the evil ;

and if these comprise such products as belong
more especially to the departments under the
care of the wife and daughters, such as eggs,
fowls, butter, and similar articles, the sympathies
of the ladies may be secured and they may become powerful auxiliaries in the good cause.

The large fields that now come out in fashionable countries are difficult to control, and interfere
considerably with their own sport, chiefly from
too great eagerness and the fear of being crowded
out when the hounds again hit off the line after
a check ; and a very interesting letter from the
famous Bramham Moor huntsman, Tom Smith,
points out clearly how such conduct interferes
with the huntsman at the moment when he
requires to concentrate his mind on the problem
of what has become of the fox. Referring to
some remarks on hunting by Mr. J. G. Elsey,
the whilom celebrated steeplechase trainer (mention of which will appear further on in this
work), he remarks :—

" He lives in a good hunting country, and has
plenty of chances of seeing the craft of hunting.
I quite agree with a lot of his remarks, and feel
sure he must take notice of hounds and their
work, which I am sorry to say the present-day
sportsman does not. It is all ride and boast
about their doings, as soon as hounds come to
a check after what we may term a quick burst ;
you can hear them talking about having jumped
such and such a place, instead of standing still
and keeping as quiet as possible until hounds
have made their cast ; and afterwards, when the
huntsman (upon hounds failing to hit off the line
themselves) begins to cast them, the field, as a
rule, instead of standing still, will ride after him

still keeping on talking, which is most annoying to the huntsman, and interferes with the hounds."

If these remarks were generally laid to heart, and acted upon, there would be fewer foxes lost, and sport in general would be greatly improved.

Q. What are the proper places for the whippers-in ?

A. " On the road the first whipper-in should be in front of the hounds, and the second whipper-in behind them ; both should keep their eyes and ears open to guard against evils, especially cur-dogs and riot." (Tom Smith.)

Q. What are their duties in the field ?

A. " When drawing big woods the first whipper-in should be forward, but not too far away from the huntsman, who is with the pack, while the second whipper-in should be handy to the huntsman, and down-wind of him, ready to afford any help that may be required. The hunt second-horsemen should be sent on to any distant points that may require watching.

" In small woods, and whin-coverts, the whippers-in should keep watch ; and, as a rule, the first whipper-in should go on with the huntsman when the hounds begin to run, leaving the second whipper-in to bring on any hounds that are behind. If, however, the fox breaks where the second whipper-in is posted, and the first whipper-in is some distance off, the second should go on temporarily with the pack, until the arrival of the first, when they should at once resume their ordinary places.

" If the huntsman is thrown out at any time by any mischance, the first whipper-in must take control in his absence, but he must be very careful in doing this or much jealousy may result.

" When a hound needs correction the whipper-in should, if possible, steal up to him and give him the thong first, and the rate afterwards. It is of little use to rate a hound well from a distance and then endeavour to get within reach to hit him.

" Similarly, when hounds have to be stopped, or turned, it is wiser to get to their heads first, and then speak to them, than to ride holloaing after them, which often seems only to confirm them in holding on, if they think they can do so with impunity."

During the course of a run, while the first whipper-in keeps near the huntsman to act according as he directs, the second should be rather behind, watching the trend of events, and ready to assist at any moment by going to a holloa, heading the fox from a drain or other stronghold, or obtaining a view when required.

When the huntsman is casting the hounds at a check the whippers-in must exercise discretion in moving hounds on after him, and should, as a rule, leave them quite alone. Many a run is lost on a bad scenting day by an officious whipper-in hurrying on a tender-nosed hound, who halts for a moment when trotting after the huntsman, thinking it has detected a whiff of scent. Many a run, too, is lost when a too-zealous youth races after and stops a hound that has cast itself rather far from the main body and picked up the scent, perhaps in the next field. He has probably had it dinned into his ears that a hound getting away by itself spoils the scent for the others, and must therefore be stopped till the main body catches it up, and he does not differentiate that in this case the others are only a couple of hundred yards away, and will catch the leader in a few seconds, as soon as ever they hear it speak to the newly-found scent. The special harm that is done is, first of all, the good hound is made to believe it has committed a fault in running the scent of the fox, for how is it to distinguish between the rate and cracks of the whip for running a hare and those now bestowed upon it for running its legitimate game ?

In the second place, when the rest of the hounds race up to where they heard their comrade running, they meet it coming back with its stern down, and a dejected look which says as plain as possible, "Look out, or you'll catch it from Bill like me!" Animals are very quick in observing signs, and taking the cue from each other, and when the pack does get on that scent there is sure to be dawdling, and a hesitancy that may last two or three fields before it wears off, and in the meantime the fox has travelled on, and the scent become very weak. If the hound, on the contrary, had been left alone, and the whipper-in had just raised his cap to draw the huntsman's attention if he was out of sight of the hound before it actually spoke to the line, the other hounds would have raced up and joined the leader with a dash that would have gone a long way towards catching the fox. Hounds never seem to settle better to a scent than when they catch up those who are pressing on before them.

To point the moral, two instances in recent years are in my mind, on both of which occasions there was quite a good scent. We had run one day about a couple of miles, the line in the last two fields being alongside a lane, which was then crossed, the fox apparently having been prevented doing so before by two cyclists, who, as is often the case, had hurried on to where they thought it likely they might view the fox. The latter's point seemed to be a park close by, near which was a village, and as the cyclists actually saw the fox go through the hedge in that direction it seemed certain it had gone there. The hounds, however, threw up at once on the other side of the fence, and at the same moment five or six hounds that had been left behind, and were being brought on by the second whip, came galloping up the lane. Instead of turning off to join the pack as they were about to do, they picked up a scent in the road, and after running it slowly for a short distance down the lane dashed off into a turnip-field on the other side, with as good a scent as there was before. The huntsman and pack were but half a small field away, while some cross-roads occurred at the end of that field and the turnip-field, so that the pack could have cut across the line of the others and joined them directly; but instead of attracting the attention of the huntsman the second whip jumped out of the lane, galloped after the hounds, and with considerable difficulty at last drove them off the line, whereupon he commenced view-holloaing and holding up his cap. The sequel was that the huntsman hurried up, the pack met some very disgusted hounds coming towards them, who absolutely refused to make any further effort, and after very desultory running on the part of the others the fox was given up, and we went to draw for another.

The other occasion was not very dissimilar. We had started with a capital scent on a very favourite line, but after running about a mile and a half there was a sudden check. There was nothing to account for it, but no doubt the fox had been headed, for while the huntsman was holding the pack on in the usual direction, a young hound came back through the fence and took up the running (but without throwing its tongue), at such a pace that the same young whip as before could not get up to him till he reached the end of a very long field. "Look at that idiot going to spoil our run!" was my comment to those with me, and sure enough he did so, for after repeating his former tactics of stopping the hound, and then view-holloaing to the huntsman, who was virtually in the same field, we crawled on for a few fields and then were obliged to give it up. It is not possible to lay to heart a few proverbial phrases, and then to apply them indiscriminately on every occasion, and meet with success!

When drawing woods with many rides in them, especially if they are wide ones, the whippers-in must be ever on the alert to prevent skirting, for some hounds get very cunning about getting a view, and prefer to use their eyes rather than their noses, and leave others to perform the more toilsome part of forcing the fox through thick covert.

Q. When a fox leaves the covert, should a holloa be given at once?

A. If the huntsman is within sight only a cap, or hat, should be raised to warn the huntsman. If the latter should be out of sight the fox should be allowed to go through the fence into the next field before a holloa is given, for fear of causing the fox to turn back.

Q. When is a likely time for a fox to break ?
A. When there is a sudden silence of the chorus, after hounds have been running him up and down the covert. They have probably been pressing him too hard to give him any opportunity of leaving, and he takes advantage of their being at fault for a moment to slip away.

Q. What instructions should the huntsman give to the second whip when on the road ?
A. That the pack must have plenty of room accorded to it, so that the hounds have time to attend to the calls of nature.

Q. Should a huntsman ever rate or strike a hound ?
A. Not for any ordinary offences, for this is the business of the whippers-in, and the hounds should look upon their huntsman as their protector and friend. At the same time in a big covert the huntsman may be the only person in a position to stop riot, and then he must, of course, act as circumstances warrant. In small provincial packs also, where there is only one whipper-in, or possibly none at all, the huntsman must perform duties that do not properly fall within his sphere.

Q. Should a huntsman constantly encourage his hounds with his voice and horn ?
A. Most certainly not, only just sufficiently to let the hounds know that he is there, and where he is. The incessant cheering of an excited huntsman soon loses its effect, or else

causes hurry and flashiness, and in either way is prejudicial.

Q. Should the huntsman use a different note when viewing a fox in covert, and going away after a fox ?

A. It is usual to sound double-tongued notes on these occasions, which the hounds soon recognise, and fly to accordingly. The late Sir Charles Slingsby used to sound the high " G " when going away, which was the most thrilling sound the writer ever heard ; but no other huntsman, as far as his knowledge goes, has ever attempted this note.

Q. Should any difference be made in the manner large and small coverts are drawn ?

A. " Large woods should always be drawn up-wind, to give hounds the advantage of getting near the fox ; but small coverts may be drawn down-wind to avoid chopping one." (Tom Smith.)

Q. Is it advisable to draw a large covert in the afternoon ?

A. Not if it is getting rather late, for there is little or no chance of forcing the fox into the open ; and since hounds must be getting tired the thick covert wearies them still more and makes them slack. Neither should a small covert be drawn when it is so late there is no chance of catching the fox before it is dark, and the probability is that they will have to be stopped when running—a thing to be avoided whenever possible. Moreover, it is a mistake to disturb a fox unless there is a chance of catching it, for the more they are disturbed the more likely they are to hide in out-of-the-way places, and are not to be found when wanted in earnest.

Q. Is any particular care required in drawing turnip-fields and such-like places ?

A. The following are the opinions of two very keen observers on this subject and cannot be more clearly stated. Mr. J. G. Elsey remarks :—

" In countries where foxes lie out a great deal, where there is more or less plough, I have noticed many a time hounds taken into a 20- or perhaps 40-acre field of high turnips, and a fox get up and be caught by view before it has gone 100, or say 200 yards, after two or three turns, and with the hounds bobbing and jumping up to get a better sight of it. Foxes, especially young foxes, will lie very close in high turnips, and have precious little chance of escape. After this has been done a few times, and, as they will tell you, hounds have been blooded, see how they will work for the rest of the season, half the pack spending most of their time during a run looking out for a view; and throwing up their heads very quickly on a cold scent, and looking up in the huntsman's face. If you want to know the harm it does for the rest of the season, think how it upsets a young setter or pointer if it sees a winged partridge jump and show itself and disappear, and repeat this several times in front of it. It takes a long time before you can get the dog not to try and catch another for itself, and a long time before it is again steady, and trusting to its nose; and are not hounds the same ? especially these pretty, racing hounds of the present day, which the huntsman is bound to ride close to, to put them right quickly as soon as they look up in his face, instead of hunting for themselves. I think it far better to let one of the whippers-in, and two or three

other horsemen, ride into the turnip-field to crack
a fox up with their whips, and then quietly, and
without hurry, lay hounds on the line."

To the above very sensible remarks Tom
Smith adds :—

"I quite agree with Mr. Elsey about drawing
turnip-fields, and should always advise not letting
hounds get a view if possible ; but a few cracks
of the whip going through the turnips should
disturb a fox, and the whipper-in at the end of
the field should put up his cap to let the
huntsman know the fox is away, and the
hounds should then be put on the line as quietly
and quickly as possible. The same remark
applies to small coverts. The less noise the better
the chance of a run. Noise only gets the
hounds' heads up, and causes them to be wild,
especially in a country full of riot."

There is a right way and a wrong way of doing
everything, and when two experts agree as to the
right method to pursue, it is wise to attend to
their advice. But how often one sees the wrong
way taken instead !

Q. In cub-hunting it is now a common practice
to let hounds run from the very commencement.
Is this a wise plan ?

A. Cub-hunting is like rehearsing for a play,
and a full-dress rehearsal—in this case a run in
the open—should not be attempted till the
performers are nearly perfect in their parts.
Unless young hounds find at first that if they
do not face the thick underwood they will have
no fun, they are not likely to become keen
drawers afterwards ; and it must be remembered
that many puppies have had no opportunity of

hunting rabbits and so forth while they were at walk, from having been brought up in towns, or at farmhouses in villages, remote from woods of any sort, and have therefore never had their faces scratched until they began cub-hunting. They have less opportunity, too, of indulging in riot without being checked in a wood than they have in a run in the open, when they may easily get separated from the pack, and can then chase hares, rabbits, or sheep to their hearts' content, without being made to suffer for it. Cub-hunting is the time when they must learn that a fox is the only quarry they are permitted to pursue, and that if they indulge in illicit amusements punishment swift and sure will quickly overtake them.

The cubs, too, have to learn what hounds mean, and that their best chance of safety is in flight; whereas if they find they escape by staying in the covert they are likely to try the same game again, when the real hunting season begins.

Q. Is it necessary for the well-being of the pack to kill cubs, or can the same end be attained by merely bustling them up?

A. All hounds soon get slack if their quarry constantly escapes them, for they expect it will do so again, and when they get into difficulties they cease to persevere. If, however, they are in the habit of being successful they cannot bear to be defeated, and will not give up till it is absolutely necessary. At the same time it is not well to kill a lot of cubs on one morning, for they are all apt to tire together, after running in covert for some time, and then can be mopped up one after the other, without benefit resulting to the hounds. If there are too many foxes it is better to stop after killing a brace, and return again a few mornings afterwards and kill another brace, and so on.

On this subject Tom Smith gives the following valuable advice :—

" The early parts of cubbing should be done in your strongest and largest woodlands for at least the first month, so that the young hounds will learn to hunt, and persevere on the line of a fox without seeing riot, and then there is little occasion for holding-up foxes ; afterwards you can commence hunting smaller coverts, in the open country.

" I always give orders for the whippers-in to let the foxes go away until the cubs have been stirred up well, for an old fox may slip away and you get away after him, and then the cubs have been left behind quite untutored.

" I am a great advocate for getting hounds well blooded during the cub-hunting season, and in fact all through the hunting season. People talk about killing too many foxes, but it is an old saying the more foxes hounds kill, the more they will have to kill. If hounds don't kill them, people will find some other means to do away with them."

Mr. J. G. Elsey's very pertinent remarks are as follows :—

" I think it wrong to whip back cubs into covert in the cubbing season, and kill them in covert ; let them break and get away if the hounds are running another fox. If, however, the fox they are running should be a cub and he also breaks, let the hounds follow him, for he will probably only journey to where he was bred, a few fields away, or may turn back again into covert on his own account. I have seen a fox, a bold cub, viewed away, and the hounds taken off another in covert and laid on the line of the bold one and kill it in three fields, which in my opinion was all wrong. I think those foxes that are bold and leave the covert are the ones to save, to show sport later on, and should not be killed before they have attained a proper age to give a run. I have noticed that those bold foxes that have been mobbed back, or rushed and killed in the open in early cub-hunting, are often very much wanted before the spring."

Q. If hounds do get away on the line of an old fox, and it is not intended to let them follow, should they be stopped at once ?

A. It is much better to let them run for a few fields until they come to a check when they can be quietly taken back, for stopping hounds is always disappointing, and discouraging to them.

Q. Is it advisable to dig a cub out if it goes to ground ?

A. Doing so occasionally teaches the young hounds to mark a fox to ground, and makes them realise they have beaten the fox.

Q. When a huntsman is blowing hounds out of covert to lay them on the scent, should he turn his horse's head towards the covert, or from it ?

A. This depends upon the circumstances of the moment. If the hounds are coming rather straggling out of a big wood, and it is necessary at first to collect them together before laying them on, the horse's head should be turned towards the wood, as the hounds are more likely then to stop and look up in the huntsman's face to see what they are to do ; but the moment there are enough to lay on the scent the horse should be turned in the direction of the line. In a small covert where the hounds should be quickly all out the horse should be turned in the right direction at once, when the first hounds will fling for the scent without dwelling, and commence to run immediately.

Q. Is it necessary to wait till all the hounds are out before they are laid on the line ?

A. This would be carrying the principle too far, for it must be remembered always that a fox is a quick travelling animal, and that the scent necessarily soon gets weak, so that every second lost means diminished scent. There is no time to wait, therefore, for the laggards of the pack, and it is sufficient to stop only the first comers until the main body joins them, when not a second should be lost in laying them on the line. If the main body are running another fox hard in covert, it is better to turn back and throw those in again who have already come out to the horn, to join the others.

Q. What usually causes a check, when running ?

A. Either the fox has got too far in front, and the scent fails ; or else it has been turned from its line by being headed by some one, or something; or it has been coursed by a wandering dog ; or the line has been foiled by sheep, or cattle.

When hunting with harriers a check is frequently caused by the sagacity of the hare, which will often retrace its steps for a long distance, and then make two or three huge bounds, and conceal itself in a furrow or some slight shelter.

If a sheep dog is seen coming slowly back towards the place where the check has occurred, it is probable that he is the culprit that is responsible for the disaster, and has been running the fox, and an early cast should be made in that direction.

The huntsman must ever be all eyes and ears during a run, keeping his attention fixed on the leading hounds, but noting all signs such as sheep wheeling ; or colts galloping a field or two ahead (for they will often chase a fox in play) ; or rooks or magpies dipping suddenly down and then shooting up again (for these birds love to mob a fox in the open) ; a coming check may thus be anticipated, and the direction indicated where a cast should be made.

Q. Should hounds always be allowed to make their own cast first ?

A. As a rule, certainly. But if the direction is clear in which the fox has gone, no time must be lost in picking up the line again. This may be managed by the huntsman moving his horse in that direction, which will probably influence the hounds to try that way, without their having to be spoken to, but if necessary a cast must be made without loss of time.

Tom Smith's dictum on this point is—

" Always allow hounds to make their own cast first, and should they fail to hit it off then make the *down-wind* cast first, unless you see something that has probably turned the fox."

The reason for this is that the hounds have

nearly always made their own cast up-wind, and therefore to do so again would be travelling twice over the same ground. Sometimes when a gale is blowing the scent is carried so far away from the actual line the fox has gone, when running sideways to the wind, the hounds travel on a parallel line a hundred yards away, and should a check then occur the fox has probably turned sharp up-wind. If he had turned down-wind he would have turned across the line the hounds are going, and they would not have lost the scent altogether but turned with him.

Q. Can anybody lay down any rules about scent ?

A. No, it is a most mysterious thing, and I quite agree with T. Smith—" Scent is one of the most uncertain things, and varies in different foxes. The state of the atmosphere has a great deal to do with it " ; and this sums up all that is known, or probably ever will be known about it. That the scent of individual foxes varies considerably there is frequent proof, and as an example a quotation may be given from my hunting diary ; it also disproves another theory that there can be no scent with a very low barometer. The pack referred to was the York and Ainsty.

" February 9, 1904. The barometer was at the ' m ' of ' stormy ' in the morning, but fell during the day to the ' S.' Wind, east, but very little of it. The ' Y and A ' met at Marston Station, and had not much scent with the first fox from Red House. A second fox crossed the green lane from Rufforth to Rufforth Whin, and there was a blazing scent, although heavy rain fell immediately the run was over." (Here follows an

account of the run, which would only be of
interest to local people.) " So we lost the fox
after a very fast run indeed. A third fox was
found at Askham Bog, but with this fox there
was very little scent."

Thus, with rain coming and an extraordinary
low glass, both of which are usually considered
absolutely fatal to scent, there was a brilliant
scent with one fox, and scarcely any with the
other two. If the second fox had not appeared on
the scene, everybody would have been content to
blame the atmospheric conditions for the lack of
scent with the other foxes.

It is usually considered that there will be a
good scent when the glass is steady, at a high
level, or is slightly rising, and a bad scent when
these conditions are reversed, but such theories
are often upset. There is certainly very seldom
a scent when a dry blue haze is in evidence, and
never when gauzy cobwebs cover all the hedges
and every blade of grass—usually seen on a
brilliant sunny morning in the autumn, and
occasionally in the spring, after a white frost
the night before. A wet mist is generally favourable to scent, and though a hard frost is by no
means inimical to it, yet when the frost is thaw-
ing, " coming out of the ground," as the country-
folk term it, there is never any scent at all.
Generally speaking, there is a better scent when
the air is somewhat colder than the ground, and
in furtherance of this it may be pointed out how
often there is a brilliant scent towards evening,
after a hot sunny day in the winter, just when
the air begins to cool, with a frost impending. It
is, however, unusual for it to be a good scenting
period unless there has been sufficient rain to

saturate the ground, penetrating right down to the subsoil.

Q. When a holloa is heard in the course of a run, and it is deemed advisable to send some one to make inquiries, what questions should he invariably ask ?

A. How long it is since the fox was seen ; which way it was coming from ; which way it was going to ; and the exact place it was last seen.

Q. What should the inquirer then proceed to do ?

A. If in view of the huntsman he should hold up his hat, and point in the direction the fox has gone, turning his horse's head in the same way. If out of sight he should give a holloa, to let the huntsman know it is all right, and hold up his hat till he can be seen. He should then ride to the place where the fox was last seen and point with his hat the way it was going. If he can be neither seen nor heard by the huntsman he should gallop back to him with the information he has acquired.

Q. If it is necessary to lift hounds, how should this be done ?

A. It is better to stop them first, and then take them quickly on, instead of starting off at a gallop, and blowing the horn to attract them to follow, which is sure to get their heads up ; then when they are wanted to hunt they only stand looking up at their huntsman-instead.

Q. What system should be followed to ensure wire being removed from the fences during the hunting season ?

A. A " wire committee " must be formed consisting both of subscribers and farmers, and after the hunt has been divided into districts, a subscriber should take charge of each, with two or three farmers under him who reside there. It is then their function to persuade their fellow-farmers to take down their wire when it is not required. If a piece has been forgotten and left up during the hunting season, notice should be sent at once to the head of the local committee, who will either go himself, or send one of his farmer assistants, to the owner of the wire with a request for its removal.

Q. How is earth-stopping carried out?
A. The old fashion of having an earth-stopper belonging to the hunt is, alas ! no longer in existence, owing to the immense increase in preserving game, and, consequently, in gamekeepers ; for the latter would not look with a friendly eye upon a stranger coming into their coverts at night ! A post-card is therefore now sent to each keeper whose beat is within the next day's draw, and he is answerable for stopping all the earths in that beat. For each night's stop he receives a fee from the hunt fund of half-a-crown. For each " find " that follows, he gets five shillings. The keepers are assembled at the end of the season, and must bring their post-cards with them to verify their claims, and they are then paid.

Q. Do they also get a reward for each litter ?
A. They get £1.

Q. How is the poultry fund managed ?
A. Some members each take a district, with a strong committee of farmers under them, similar to the wire committee. When a claim is sent in

the member in whose district it is forwards it to one of the farmers of the committee, who at once investigates the claim (if the member does not do so himself), and marks on the claim the amount thought to be reasonable.

Q. Are false or frivolous claims often sent in ?
A. Sometimes they are very ludicrous ! The writer has known claims sent in for pigs, ewes, calves, foals, and once even for a sick cow that had died !

It is a great boon to a hunt if they possess some shrewd, practical member, one who would have succeeded at the Bar if he had been fated to enter that profession, and who can put his finger at once upon the weak spot in the chain of evidence.

On one occasion a claim was sent in for twenty fowls that were stated to have been taken by a fox, whereupon the member for the district went over to inquire into the claim. On arriving at the farm he took the opportunity, before he entered the house, to count the fowls he saw running about, and then went in to interview the farmer's wife. "How many chickens had you," he inquired, "before the fox took them ? " whereupon the dame answered, "One hundred." "And," said he, producing a letter from his pocket, "the fox took twenty, did he not? " "Yes," replied the dame. "That's all right, then," said her visitor, "I am so glad to be able to tell you your chickens have come back again, for I have just counted a hundred outside the house ! Good morning."

On another occasion the same envoy investigated a claim for eleven fat fowls, and on arriving at the farm he asked if they would show him the place where the fox had caught the victims, which was readily agreed to. When they got to the place he saw the remains of a nest and some egg-shells, and beginning to get suspicious he asked whether the fox had taken full-grown birds or chickens. The reply was, " A hen and chickens." He next inquired if it was eggs or chickens the fox had taken ; whereupon the man confessed it was a hen sitting on eggs the fox had caught, but the eggs would probably have hatched out all right and grown up into good marketable poultry, so the hunt ought to pay for them as such. "Well," said the other, " I have often heard of *counting* chickens before they were hatched, but I never heard of their being *paid for* before ! "

Though foxes undoubtedly are destructive, a very great deal is laid to their charge undeservedly, and all the sins committed by wandering dogs and cats are heaped on their devoted heads. It is rather curious that gamekeepers are so abusive of them, when they are the best friends possible to a lazy or incompetent man, for, like the domestic cat, they bear the blame for all shortcomings, which would be laid on the right shoulders if they were improved out of existence !

CHAPTER IV

STAGS

HUNTING wild stags on Exmoor has become of late years extremely popular, and with the increase in the public taste for the sport, a corresponding increase has fortunately taken place in the number of wild red-deer, chiefly owing to the estimation in which they are held, and the decrease in poaching which formerly took place. So much have they increased that though at one time it looked possible that even the famous Devon and Somerset Staghounds might have to be given up through lack of deer, there are now three packs in addition, the Quantock, Sir John Amory's, and the Barnstaple, each of which find ample game to hunt.

There is a glamour about wild stag-hunting that appeals to the heart of most, savouring as it does of a knowledge of woodcraft that at any rate, if required, is not so much in evidence in other forms of hunting in the British Isles. The method pursued is now pretty generally understood. The harbourer, a picturesque figure in the mind of the public, has to be up betimes that he may, if possible, view the stags as they return to covert after feeding ; but should he be unsuccessful in this, he must then search the ground carefully till he meets with the signs of a goodly stag, and then locate where he has taken up his abode for the day, and bring the information to the huntsman, that he may know where to rouse a quarry fit to hunt. The tufters next appear upon the scene, a few staunch old hounds that can be trusted, whose business it is to rouse the stag, and force him out of the covert, when the rest of the pack, which has been shut up in a stable not far away, is brought rapidly up, laid upon the scent, and the chase of the stag begins in earnest.

This sounds all very simple, and occasionally no doubt is so. But there is many a slip in hunting as well as drinking, and long hours may sometimes be passed before the hounds are fleeting over picturesque Exmoor, and your good steed is doing his generous best to carry you up and down hill, through mire and waste, disregarding in the excitement the pricking of that dwarf gorse with which the heather of the Devonshire moors is so plentifully intermingled, while a watchful eye is ever kept for signs denoting the whereabouts of a treacherous bog.

The harbourer's duty is no light one, and he must be well versed in the appearance of the slot, and other signs, not to make a mistake as to the age of the deer he has harboured, or whether it is a hind or a stag. He must not be careless either, and overlook his exit from the covert, thinking all the time the stag is safely lying down within, when he is already miles away in another direction.

A cunning old stag, which has been hunted before, perhaps many times, is not always willing to face the open, and trust to his heels for escape, and may give the tufters much trouble before they can persuade him to leave the covert. So long as there is another deer within hail, a hind possibly or a younger stag, the hunted one is very apt to try to shift the tufters on to it, sometimes indeed poking it out of the spot where it is lying down, and taking its place himself.

Q. How many calves does a hind usually have at a birth ?

A. Seldom more than one.

Q. How are deer of different ages colloquially spoken of ?

A. As a two, three, or four year-old "galloper," "old stags," and "heavy deer." They count "the rights" also, "Brow, Bay, and Tray, and so many points on top."

Q. How old should a stag be before it is hunted ?

A. Four years old at least; though by accident, or for lack of another, it sometimes happens that a three-year-old is run.

Q. When does stag-hunting begin ?

A. Bye-days, somewhat analogous to cub-hunting, begin about July 25th, sometimes rather earlier ; and the opening meet of the Devon and Somersetshire Staghounds takes place at Cloutsham, usually about August 8th.

Stags are hunted till the middle of October, when hounds are stopped for about three weeks, and then hind-hunting begins and goes on till April, when stags are again hunted till early in May.

Q. What are favourite places to stay at for stag-hunting ?

A. Minehead, Porlock, Lynton (the two latter places are near the Doone Valley, so celebrated through Blackmore's romantic story of " Lorna Doone "), and Dulverton are all within easy reach of most of the meets, while there are several scattered inns and farmhouses, where lodgers are taken in and made very comfortable.

Q. Is it necessary for a stranger to take his own horses, or can hunters be hired on the spot ?

A. It is far bettter to hire, as several persons have gone into the business, and let out large numbers of good hunters by the day, or for a longer period as desired.

Q. Do wild stags give longer runs than carted ones ?

A. Both often give long runs, but with a carted stag there is none of that indescribable feeling there is in the chase of a wild animal, though there is much to be said in favour of the former when no other hunting can be obtained. It is often a subject of remark, that staghounds after a carted deer do not go with the same dash at first as foxhounds after a fox, but they cover a distance of eight or ten miles in much shorter time than foxhounds do.

It has also frequently been said that staghounds seem only really to settle down, just at the time when foxhounds would be thought to have had a first-rate run indeed, after some ten miles have been covered, if they have a first-class stag before them.

Q. Are not the Ward Union a famous pack of staghounds ?

A. Yes, most deservedly so, and they have a splendid country to ride over. At the time that the late Empress of Austria was hunting from Summerhill in Meath the Wards had one of their most famous deer, the " Enfield Doe." It used to be said she had never been taken under fifteen miles, and usually the runs she gave were much longer. The writer has two runs marked on his hunting-map after this famous hind, in the first of which she was turned out at " The Black Bull," and after crossing the well-known Bush farm she left Dunshaughlin about a mile to the left, went past Gerrardstown, and was taken near Boyne View, about a mile from Navan, a distance of nineteen miles in an absolutely straight line on the map, and of course much more as the hounds went.

On the other occasion, on March 5, 1879, the Enfield Doe was turned out at Norman's Grove, and after crossing Fairy-house, left Ratoath some two miles to the right, then swinging round by Tobergregan House she passed over Garristown Hill, and leaving Bellewstown to the right was taken within two miles of Duleek. This run was slightly over fourteen miles in a straight line on the map, from the starting-point to the end, but it was a twisting run, so a good many more miles were traversed. In neither run was there a check to speak of; we were galloping all the way. The writer assisted to take the Enfield Doe on each occasion, and rode a five-year-old English mare by Speculum, that had only been ridden in a flying country, and had never seen a bank in her life till she came to Ireland the previous October. The late Lord Randolph Churchill took keen interest in watching the mare being trained to

jump banks, and used to come and help to lead
her over the country in a lunging-rein, till she
began to understand how to do them properly.
A month after the Norman's Grove run Kittiwake
ran second at Punchestown ridden by the late
Colonel Wardrope ; and the next year she won
the same race beating thirteen other runners, after
having been out with the Ward hounds sixteen
times that season.

The late excellent sportsman, Mr. Leonard
Morrogh, was then at the head of the Wards, and
he one day mentioned how important ivy was to
the well-being of deer in a paddock. It seems to be
an excellent tonic for them.   He also pointed out
a very simple but very wise contrivance to induce
the deer to take sufficient exercise to be fit for the
exertion of a long chase. All animals if they
have sufficient space keep constantly moving for
the greater part of the twenty-four hours, but
they soon get tired of doing so in a place so
limited they can see all round it.   Barriers were
therefore erected in the deer paddock so as to
obstruct the view there, and into the sheds, the
consequence being the deer were always full of
curiosity to know what was going on on the *other*
side, and continually moved across to see; but no
sooner had they done so than they thought there
might be something going on after all where they
had just left, so back they went again for fear of
missing the fun. They were therefore kept in
good, hard condition, whereas if they had been
able to see into every corner they would have
just stood still, and got fat and soft.

Q. How long rest does a deer require after
a chase, before being fit to come out again?

A. It depends so much as to the severity of the run. Some deer are only " twenty-minutes' deer," and then give up, often going into a farm-yard or stable when they have had enough, and such, of course, do not require anything like so long a rest as an animal like the Enfield Doe, such deer requiring about six weeks before coming out again. The "twenty-minutes' heroes " are very useful for the first days after a frost, when horses —and riders—have somewhat lost condition.

Q. Is it not difficult to capture deer after a run ?

A. Yes, and it may be a dangerous thing to attempt if a person does not understand how to do it, and keep a sharp look-out. Though the stags have been deprived of their horns they can strike very sharply with their fore-hoofs, and may inflict a serious wound. Seizing an opportunity a whip-thong should be cast round the animal's neck and firmly held, while a willing assistant approaches from behind and slips his hand inside the cheek of the deer. When two persons have hold of either cheek the animal can be fairly easily controlled, and led in the required direction. The knuckles sometimes get cut against the back-teeth, if the deer struggles much.

Q. As a tame deer cannot know the country where it is turned out, what guides it in making a point ?

A. A deer frequently makes for a hill, if it can see one in the distance, otherwise it usually runs cheeking the wind. They are very fond of the society of cows, and if any are in the fields the deer will usually diverge to them, frequently stopping with them and grazing till the hounds get near ; they often, indeed, wait there till the hounds get a view.

As an instance of what a wild stag is capable of, the account of a run which took place in Yorkshire on March 8, 1865, may be read with interest. The stag probably had escaped from a park, but he had been living in the district for a considerable time, first in the neighbourhood of Castle Howard, and then round Newburgh Park, and to all intents and purposes was a wild stag. At that time there was in existence a pack of staghounds, formerly harriers, that were kept by some very sporting farmers in the neighbourhood of Easingwold, and I am indebted to Captain Frank Reynard for the following account :—

" 'Lord Nunburnholme,' so christened on the 9th of March, 1865, was first hunted by the Easingwold Staghounds on the 25th of February that year, when he was found on Yearsley Moor, between Gilling Castle and Newburgh Park, and hunted down to Bossall wood, close to Aldby Park, in Lord Middleton's country, after a run of about twenty-five miles.

" It was a keen morning on the 8th of March, with snow visible on the tops of the wolds, and the hounds having laid out overnight at Lobster House (on the York and Malton road), found the stag in Bossall wood, which went away past Willow Bridge, by Crambe, to Kirkham Abbey Station ; being headed here he turned into Howsham wood, and from there ran through Westow churchyard, on to Eddlethorpe, past Burythorpe, and so to Birdsall. From here he turned, leaving Wharram on the left, to Burdale, where he endeavoured to take shelter in a shed on Mr. North's farm, but being driven out by two cur-dogs, he went up the Fridaythorpe Valley ; then heading for Sledmere he reached Fimber Station, where the snow lay three inches deep, and went over Huggate Wold, past Warter, and was eventually taken at Mr. Wilberfoss Hornby's farm on Nunburnholme Wold. Time of the run, four hours and thirty-five minutes. The distance is put at about forty miles.

" The names of those who were present when the deer was taken are as follows, only seven remaining out of a field of three hundred—and all members of the Easingwold Hunt :

" Mr. John Batty (Master of the Staghounds), Thornton Baxby, Easingwold.

" Mr. Robert Batty, Tollerton.

" Mr. John Cotes, Peep o'Day, Easingwold.

" Mr. James Batty, Stillington.

" Mr. Thomas Batty, Aldwark.

" Mr William Wright, Stillington.

" Mr. Samuel Swales, Tollerton.

" The following four got within one mile of the point where the deer was taken :

" Mr. Gerald Walker, Sand Hutton.

" The Rev. F. Simpson, Foston.

" Mr. John Ellerby, Terrington.

" Mr. William Barber, Easingwold.

" The deer was christened by the ladies of Mr. Wilberfoss Hornby's household ' Lord Nunburnholme ' on the morning of March the 9th, 1865, on which day he and the hounds and what horses remained, went by rail from Market Weighton to Alne."

One of the most remarkable features of this great run, which, starting on the plain near York, afterwards traversed nearly the whole of the

wolds, is that Mr. Robert Batty rode eighteen
stone, and yet got to the end of the chase. He
was a fine horseman, but a big, burly man, and
the extraordinary horse that carried him so
bravely that day was a long low chestnut, almost
thoroughbred, by Gray President, dam by Bolus,
but stood only fifteen hands one inch in height.
He had been fired on both hocks, but was perfectly sound, and no matter how fast, or how far
hounds ran, Robert Batty was always at the tail
of the pack. He was often asked to put his
own price on the horse, but nothing would
tempt him to part with his favourite, and I
believe he kept him to the end of his life.

We must now leave the consideration of " Brow,
Bay, and Tray," the glory of the West, and
proceed to discuss the far more generally distributed chase of the fox—which brings such
brightness into the lives of its followers, both high
and low, every succeeding winter.

CHAPTER V

FOXES

THERE is some mysterious attraction about a fox, some element that causes intense agitation in the beholder whenever one is seen, quite apart from the excitement of the chase ; which is not caused, for instance, by the sight of a hare, though that animal is much prized in a harrier country. What this influence is I cannot explain, but until the fox disappears again from view it invariably monopolises the attention of every one who sees it. From one's nursery days one has heard tales of " Brer Fox," of his cunning, his wit, and adroitness in taking care of himself, and in getting the better of those with whom he is associated, and perhaps this throws a halo round him, that after-years spent in his pursuit seem still further to accentuate. As a means of providing pleasure there is nothing to compare with him, for while a single fox is capable of affording the keenest enjoyment to a whole host of people, a single pheasant would provide but a momentary pleasure to the man who shot it ; while it would cause feelings of envy and disappointment to the rest, if it was the only bird to be found that day !

Mr. J. G. Elsey has favoured me with the following observations, the result of long experience when watching foxes at home and at their ease, which will, I am sure, afford as much pleasure to others as they have done to myself :—

" Foxes are really very interesting animals, and there is much to be learned by studying their habits. I find by experience I can nearly always tell for certain whether I have a litter of cubs anywhere on my place by looking round about the 14th to the 20th May. They are especially easy to tell after a heavy dew or slight rain.

" By the date mentioned the cubs in this part of the world (Lincolnshire) begin to paddle about outside the hole, and tread flat the mouth of it, and a little of the surrounding herbage, but if you are in doubt take note if there is a blue-bottle or two buzzing in and out of the earth ! In a few days it will be plain to see if cubs are really there, for there will soon be parts of rats, their skins, and perhaps a few feathers to go by ; and then several young rabbits, or their mangled remains, will be found, and even a dead field mouse or two as well.

" Old Foxy Todd, a fox-keeper of Mr. Chaplin when he hunted this part of the Blankney country when I was a boy, (Foxy Todd still lives near here), tells me that when he had several litters to look after and to count the cubs, he used to be near the earth where the litter was very early in the morning, almost before it was light, and see what the old foxes would bring the cubs, both dog and vixen in most cases helping to feed the family. It was wonderful how hard they worked for the cubs, bringing them five times their requirements, and varying from a turkey to a young thrush or blackbird, or a rat. He says he had his good days and his bad days in those early mornings.

"Foxes in this country generally leave the earth about the 21st to 28th June, and go into a wheat or bean field somewhere near. When the wheat or beans are high you can usually tell where they are by looking for their playground in and out through the hedges, near where they have taken up their abode in the field.

"If you notice their droppings you cannot, as a rule, help noticing many beetle wings and bodies. Foxes and cubs eat many beetles, and it is very amusing to watch cubs late in the evening when they come out about 8.30 to 9.30. If still light enough to see them on the grass, if there is any near the earth, they may be seen to pounce on and catch scores of beetles, varying their beetling by gambolling and rearing up at each other, and rolling over each other like kittens.

"I have seen an old vixen when cubs are getting a fair size send them back from following her, more than a hundred yards. If a vixen sees you, or smells, or hears you when the cubs are out, she will give an angry sound like 'gwo, gwo,' and the cubs will rush into the earth as fast as they can scud, and probably you will not see them again for at least an hour ; if well away from the earth herself the vixen will not follow them, but scout round, and then go through a hedge and be no more seen for some time. I have seen this near the artificial earth, where, however, cubs are seldom born, but are nearly always brought there when very young, after being disturbed elsewhere, and they then remain till about June 28th.

"Nearly every year it is the same, but I am inclined to think this year they were either born in the earth, or else brought there at once ; but it has not been so in other years. I believe most cubs are born in a hole opened out, or scratched by the vixen in the spring, and seldom in an artificial earth.

"If there are rabbits enough for plenty of food foxes generally keep within a few miles of where they were bred, and when hounds are after them, certainly for the first season, they will run past, or round, or go to ground where they were born. I have known one old fox stay about until his fifth season, beating hounds many times, but they killed him at last after a very fast run, the pace beating him, and I now have his head. I knew him well from a cub, and so also did several men about the place.

"It is difficult to tell a run fox from a fresh one when hunting, but I can always do so for certain if I can get a look at the fox before he knows he is observed. Then he puts on a spurt, and is a different animal to all appearance in a moment, although if very tired he soon settles down to a beaten gait again.

"It seems to me more foxes lie out in the fields than used to be the case, probably owing to so much game being reared, and consequent shooting in woods and coverts ; or else because it may be that the foxes bred in the open have a better chance of growing up, and that these remain in the open fields."

These remarks from a very keen observer are well worth attention. A fox-cub's *menu* is a very varied one, and moles, frogs, rats, water-hens, young rooks, and many other items all enter into it.

Mr. Elsey's statement of the advantage it is to see a fox before it sees you, to determine whether it is the run one or not, is very true. When a tired fox puts on a momentary spurt he goes very like a fresh one, but he cannot keep it up, and he soon resumes his former shambling gait, so characteristic of the beaten animal. There are few hunting-men, however, who are sufficiently close observers to be absolutely trustworthy about a fox being the run one, as many a huntsman knows to his cost! When he can put confidence in the person giving the information it is an immense help to him, as the following anecdote may serve to show; it also illustrates the rapidity with which a first-rate huntsman can grasp the situation, and make up his mind what course to pursue :—

We had been running a fox for about thirty-five minutes with Lord Middleton's hounds, when they dashed across the bridge at Kirkham Abbey and up the hill past the venerable ruins, the scent having been first-rate all the way. Fortunately the fox made a little detour in the direction of Howsham wood, which enabled my somewhat tired horse to keep inside the circle, and arrive at the top of the hill at the same time as the leading hounds; as we did so there was a holloa only some two fields ahead, and toward it the hounds flew on the scent, with redoubled energy. Grant, the huntsman, was a few lengths behind, while being still on rising ground he could not see so far around as I could, when suddenly the merest glimpse of a dead-beaten fox dragging himself through a gap in the hedge of a field, at right angles to the direction we were going, flashed across me. "Grant," I shouted, "they are on a fresh fox! There goes ours," pointing with my whip, as I spoke. "Are you certain?" he replied as we galloped on. "Absolutely certain," was my answer, whereupon he wheeled his horse to the right, and blew his horn with all his might, though the pack were already racing at their best pace in the next field, straight toward the man in the distance, who kept holloaing with full lung-power. Grant, however, took no notice of him, but kept on blowing his horn until the whipper-in had managed to get to the hounds, and sent them straggling back to the horn. Now came an anxious moment, for hounds whipped off when running hard do not often settle down very kindly to another scent, especially as in this case, it was sure to be weak, with such a beaten fox in front. To my relief, however, the pack at once started running, directly they touched the place where the fox was viewed, and as at the end of that very field he had lain down to rest, on jumping up in view he was rolled over at once. Grant's "Thank you, sir, I should never have got him if it had not been for you," fell on very gratified ears; at the same time I felt the real credit was due to Grant himself for so quickly solving the problem, when every appearance was in favour of the pack having been right before, they never having been off the burning scent for even a moment, and no indication having been given of a change of foxes.

To the following questions Tom Smith, the

Bramham Moor huntsman, has kindly given the result of his experience in the answers to them :—

Q. What is the usual number in a litter of cubs ?

A. "The average number is about six or seven, though there are several instances of vixens having as many as nine, or occasionally twelve or thirteen."

Q. Are there different breeds of foxes in different localities ?

A. "There are what is termed the greyhound fox, which is like a Scotch-bred or moorland fox. Then there is the stub-bred fox, which is bred above ground. And lastly the terrier fox, which is of a smaller breed, but none the less shows as much sport as any other, and is often stouter."

Q. What is the ordinary weight of dog foxes and vixens ?

A. "The average weight of a dog fox is about 12 lbs., and many vixens weigh as much ; but both sexes vary."

Q. When should the earths be stopped, and how should this be done ?

A. "In the short days earths ought to be stopped soon after dark, whilst the fox is out feeding. In the spring, when vixens are in cub, earths should be left till morning, if they are used for breeding.

"A good method for stopping an earth is to have a well-made whin kidd, that will fit closely into it."

Q. Do you recommend artificial earths ?

A. "Yes, they are very necessary for many

reasons, and when coverts and the country are often disturbed, foxes lie freely in them, and can easily be bolted when wanted."

Q. What is the probable cause of mange appearing in a country hitherto free from it?

A. "It is contributed mainly through imported foxes; but also in big shooting districts where the old foxes are destroyed, and the cubs brought up by hand, unnatural food and neglected attention are great factors in inducing mange."

Q. Do badgers and foxes agree together? Will the old sow badger kill fox-cubs?

A. "Foxes and badgers do not agree, though they have been known to occupy the same earth, in separate chambers. I do not think a badger will kill a fox-cub, but they will take possession of an earth where there is a litter of cubs, and banish the foxes."

When stopping earths it must always be borne in mind that the material used should permit of ventilation, or a fox may be suffocated within, and especially should this be seen to when a fox has gone to ground after a run, when he requires more air than at ordinary times. On such occasions, if the hiding-place is a small and confined one, it should not be long before the stopping is taken out again altogether. When the same hole has to be frequently stopped it is necessary to have something handy on the spot, which can be quickly inserted, and quickly removed, but when not in use it should be concealed, lest some unauthorised person should see it and be tempted to make undue use of it. Small faggots (or " kidds ") are excellent for this

purpose ; and some wire netting rolled into this
shape makes as good a tool as anything else, and
will last for years if carefully laid by when not
required.

One of the late Sir Charles Slingsby's maxims
(the famous Master and huntsman of the York and
Ainsty, who was drowned in the terrible hunting
accident at Newby Ferry on February 4, 1869)
was that a blown fox always lies down as soon
as he can find an opportunity of getting out of
sight ; while a fox that has caught his second
wind, but is getting beaten, struggles on as long
as he can possibly do so. The first fox, for
instance, lies down on reaching a covert within
ten yards of the hedge, but the other fox will go
well into the wood before he stops, and even
then generally keeps moving about. The pursuing hounds most often flash over the blown fox,
dashing on into the covert expecting the fox has
gone on, and thus giving him an opportunity,
frequently availed of, of slipping back the way
he came in as soon as he has recovered his wind ;
while the hounds either rouse a fresh fox and
change on to him, or else are so long in coming
back the scent has grown stale in the meantime,
and our cunning friend is given up. In the
same way a blown fox seldom goes far into an
earth or hole, as he knows he must have plenty
of air ; but the tired fox can do with less, and
goes further into the haven of refuge as soon as
he has reached it. I have more than once, when
a fox has been suddenly lost after a racing ten or
fifteen minutes, proceeded to search all the rabbit
holes in the vicinity large enough for a fox to
get into, and seen the tip of its brush sticking out
of the one he was in, though as soon as he knew

he was observed he has at once struggled on far
into the hole. I have repeatedly, too, known
a fox just save his brush by dashing into a small
hole, or drain, and in a few minutes dash out
again, even while we were still there, from
finding he was suffocating from want of air.

A verification of Sir Charles's theory often
recurs to my mind, though it is, alas! thirty
years ago since the run took place. It was one
of those mornings when the scent serves so well
the hounds race as if they were in view, and a
fox never gets a chance of getting his second
wind if the pack get away close behind his brush.
I happened to be riding Kettleholder, a horse
that had been heavily backed for the Cambridgeshire, and also for the Hunt Cup at Ascot, and
therefore possessed of great speed, whilst he was
an excellent and very sure fencer. With such a
horse to ride, and grass all the way, and with no
fear of " the dreaded wire " in those halcyon
days, it mattered little how fast the hounds went,
and when after some fifteen minutes we jumped
into a large grass field at the further end of
which stretched a long belt of wood, fringing the
bank of a river, the fox was barely half way
across, straining every nerve to reach the haven
that lay in front. Though the hounds did not
actually see the fox, they were running as fast as
if they did so, and it was an interesting problem
whether they would reach him or not before he
could gain the wood ; but he managed to struggle
safely into it, the chorus of the pack kept up for
fifty yards or so as they dashed through the
brush-wood, and then there was sudden silence.
Mindful of the lessons I had learned from Sir
Charles, I galloped to the exact spot where the

fox had gone through the wood-hedge, and sat there till the huntsman at length came up. Had he been Sir Charles, the fox would have had but a short shrift, but when I remarked that the fox had gone in there, and I was certain he was lying down close by, I received but a growl in reply; and much annoyed at having been left so far behind in such a brilliant gallop, the huntsman jumped into the wood and went down the nearest ride. Presently I heard his voice receding farther and farther away, and at length in about twenty minutes time he proceeded to blow the hounds out at the further end of the covert, never having touched on the scent at all. Two or three companions had remained with me, so before leaving the place I said to them, "Just let's see if the fox is not here all the time," and jumping into the wood I was beginning to search the long grass and thorns at its edge, when up jumped the fox, which had not been five yards from us all the time. We gave no sign, and let him crawl away, for as the huntsman had refused to be helped, and had fairly lost his fox, we thought the latter should not have an unfair advantage taken now over him, after he had given such a gallant run.

Sometimes a fox may be seen during a run sitting up on his haunches, gravely looking back at his pursuers. If he should wait till they have approached comparatively near before he moves off, depend upon it he has some well-considered plan of escape in his mind, most likely a safe refuge hard by. Certainly it is odds against handling that fox unless his schemes are upset by something other than the hounds themselves. He would not be so confident if he was not sure he could defeat the pack, and escape. Most often, however, it is a newly-disturbed fox that thus behaves, and care must be taken not to change foxes on such an occasion.

Foxes are very good climbers, and can ascend a high wall if there are any interstices between the bricks through the mortar perishing and falling out. They are often, too, astonishing tree-climbers, and can ascend a rough-barked tree, like an elm, to a very great height indeed. About thirty years ago there was always a fox to be seen nearly at the top of a lofty old elm in Newby Park, near Ripon, which used to make the upper branches his daylight abode, above the height at which the stable lads could annoy him by throwing stones. Foxes often pass the day in snug places amongst ivy ; and many will still re-member a day at Hawkhills, in Yorkshire, when three foxes were found in fir-trees at the same time in the same wood.

Whether badgers really do harm in a fox-hunting country is an often-debated question; but there is little doubt that, if a badger desires the room of a fox rather than his company, it will certainly have its own way, and in some countries badgers are very prevalent. At the annual dinner of the keepers and earth-stoppers of Lord Middleton's hunt held at Malton on the Derby Day of 1902, it was stated to the assembled company that one hundred and fifty badgers had been killed within the limits of the hunt in the two previous years.

Badgers are sometimes accused of killing fox-cubs, but no satisfactory evidence has ever been published of this ; and the badger is such a quaint survival of our ancient British fauna, it would be a pity to exterminate him on insufficient grounds. Perhaps some of the real culprits have been foxes themselves, for a vixen with young cubs will not tolerate those of even her dearest friend, and if they intrude she just gives them a snap on the top of their heads, and cracks their skulls!

Mr. Elsey's letter on the subject of badgers, foxes, and cats, is given *in extenso* as follows :—

" Few people thought we had either badgers or otters in this neighbourhood, yet my old terrier drove a badger out of my artificial earth in front of hounds, and he weighed 30 lbs. Also when the Bucks Otter Hounds came to the small river, the Bain, they quickly found the scent of, and killed, an otter ; and again this season they killed two otters in another small stream at Somerby, when few people thought or believed there were any about. A badger that has got first possession of an artificial earth will keep it clear of foxes ; and so also will a cat ! This is my own experience. I have had to bolt and kill two or three cats out of my earth, and had no foxes there while a cat was in possession, though several were about, which very quickly took to lying in the earth again after the cats were killed."

Mr. Elsey has perfected an extremely successful plan of an artificial fox-earth, the details of which he kindly furnished me with some years ago, and which has proved very successful elsewhere than in its original home. (It is best made in duplicate, so that, when bolting foxes, those that first come out can be allowed to escape into Box No. 2.)

Clay is the best soil for an artificial earth, as

rabbits cannot scratch in, or foxes scratch out, as they can in sandy soil.

One set of pipes should debouch into the side of a ditch, so that a fox hunting up it will easily find the entrance.

The other set of pipes must have the mouth well screened from observation by bushes, dead thorns, or something similar, so that a fox can emerge without being seen, or there will be great difficulty in bolting him. It is preferable for this set of pipes to terminate in a hollow in the

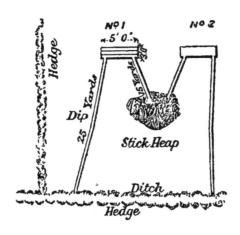

ground, or a shallow pit, which helps to hide it, and in which the bushes can be heaped. Some skill is required in adjusting these, for they should be so arranged as to afford shelter to a fox when driven out of the earth, to allow him to recover from the first dazzling effect of the daylight, and to have a chance of making up his mind where he will go, while all the time he has to dodge the terrier which has followed close after him, and is chasing him round and round. A few tree-roots, trunks of worthless trees, large rocks, or anything similar that is handy may be thrown loosely together on the ground, then some large branches heaped on the top of them, and finally dead thorns or sticks of any description piled high up, when a complete shelter will have been made that should satisfy the requirements of any fox.

It may here be remarked that the slit to which a fox's eye contracts in daylight differs from the similar slit in a cat's eye, the former being nearly horizontal and the latter perpendicular.

If the earth is not situated in a wood there must be a convenient hedge by which the fox can approach the entrance to the earth, and depart, without being observed, or the scheme will prove a failure.

Water must be close at hand.

If there is any fear of damp getting in, supplementary drains must be cut to prevent it, for foxes will not lie in a damp kennel. No situation should be selected where there is a chance of any flood entering the pipes from the ditch.

It is only on very rare occasions that an artificial earth ought to be stopped, as foxes should learn to regard it as a sanctuary, available at all times. They do not mind being bolted from it any number of times, but dislike being stopped out when they need its shelter.

The earth itself consists of a wooden box, very near the surface so that it can easily be opened and cleansed, out of which two sets of pipes proceed, which should be so arranged that a fox can easily escape out of the other, if an assailant enters by one of them ; but which he can also defend at advantage if he so prefers. When all the conditions are to its liking a fox takes very kindly to such an earth, and they answer very well, sometimes miles away in a bare country far from a covert of any description. One person alone should have charge of them, and be empowered to bolt the foxes from time to time to teach them to leave at once when the hounds are there, so that there is then no wearisome wait while the terrier is baying the fox.

The wooden box forming the kennel should be the size and shape of an ordinary hearthrug, about five feet long by three broad. It must not be *more* than fifteen inches high—so that a fox cannot sit up inside it and foul it. A little dry sand may be scattered over the bottom to facilitate cleansing it.

The top of the box should be about two feet under ground. There must be a slight fall given to the pipes from the box. There may be a false bottom to the box, with rope handles to it, so that it can be easily lifted out if necessary at the annual inspection, and cleansed.

The pipes should open into the box from opposite ends of one of the long sides, so that if a terrier should stop and bay at one entrance the fox can bolt without having to pass the dog, which it would have to do if the apertures were close together. They must not, however, be exactly opposite each other, lest they act like a chimney, and create a draught. By keeping them at each end of one of the long sides a large space is formed free of draught, to make a sleeping chamber.

The boards forming the lid must go on lengthways of the box, so that when the board covering the two entrances of the pipes is lifted off these will be at once exposed. This board should be left loose, but the others may be nailed down.

Each set of pipes should be about forty-five yards, including to and from the box. Such a length deters a wandering dog from investigating the vulpine sanctuary. Sanitary pipes should be used about eleven inches in diameter; a fox is then obliged to go outside for the wants of nature, instead of staying inside if the weather is stormy, and defiling the pipes. They should be laid with a dip in the middle, to prevent draught.

The mouth of each pipe should terminate in a strong wooden frame so contrived that an iron grating can be dropped down from the top to close the entrance, which will yet admit plenty of air to a blown fox.

The bottom of the grating should rest on wood to prevent a fox from scratching out. Foxes also prefer to enter over a wooden floor rather than through a bare pipe.

The last three or four feet should be laid level, or if any slant is given it should be slightly downwards, so that a fox can rest easily while taking observations before leaving the earth. A natural earth almost always takes this course. It is a good plan to heap clay over the lid of the box, to make it impervious to rain.

The earth should be examined once a year in the spring, when it will probably be untenanted for a while, as a vixen usually goes elsewhere to drop her cubs. Sometimes it may be found that damp has got in, when steps must be immediately taken to correct this, or the earth will be deserted by foxes. Sometimes also a dead fox may be found inside, that has met with some disaster and has crawled here to die. As a rule, however, if everything is normal, nothing will be found except a few old dry bones, which are easily removed, and should be at once taken away.

When bolting a fox from the earth for the hounds to pursue, it is advisable that there should be two persons present, one presiding over the exit of the drain where the terrier is, and the other over the entrance to the second earth, for if there are several foxes inside, it is not reasonable to have them all running about the country together. When the first fox bolts into the stick heap, if the terrier is still at another fox inside the first-comer should be allowed to pass on into the duplicate earth ; and each fox in succession should be allowed to follow suit, until at length the terrier follows on the heels of the last fox. Each watcher— who, of course, must be carefully concealed from the fox—should then immediately push down his slide, thus preventing the fox from following his playmates, or returning to the old earth ; he is in consequence forced to give a run. When another fox is wanted, and is safe inside the second earth, he can be called upon in due time to take a share in the day's sport.

Q. What soil should be chosen for planting with gorse ?

A. Strong rather than sandy soil, for then it is not easy for foxes to make earths in the gorse, which are often a trouble when the covert has grown thick.

Q. Should a whole field be given up to gorse ?

A. It should rather be divided into two parts, with a wide division between the two, so that one part can be burned down when necessary, and the other half left to provide shelter till

No. 1 is high enough again to do so. The second half can then be burned down in its turn. Gorses are often made so large there is considerable difficulty in forcing foxes to leave them; and by dividing them into two parts this danger is much reduced.

Q. When should gorse be burned or cut down ?

A. When it is so old it has become hollow underneath, and becomes distasteful to foxes from being draughty, and not affording sufficient shelter.

Q. Is the practice of turning out foxes detrimental to pheasants and partridges, while they are sitting ?

A. No, they do practically no harm then.

Q. How can this be ? Gamekeepers are apt to say just the reverse.

A. A little reflection will show the reason of this statement. No M.F.H. would think of turning out an old fox, for it would at once try to make away towards its own home, though if it came from a long distance this would probably be futile. It would, however, be unlikely to settle down where it was turned out. Most cubs are dropped in March, so that even if they were turned loose in May or June, they would be too young to harm sitting game. Cubs of that tender age, moreover, are too small to look after themselves, and are kept in confinement, and fed artificially until they have grown enough to have a fair chance of getting their own living; which, however, will have to be supplemented for some time with rabbits, wood-pigeons, rats, or small birds, shot for them to supplement their dinners.

It is this keeping them so long in confinement that is such a prevalent cause of mange.

Q. Can any method of confining cubs be suggested as likely to prevent mange appearing ?

A. The most likely way to cause it is to keep them in a stable, or other outhouse, where they are ever in an unnatural state. Every effort should be made instead to copy the conditions which would be natural to them if they were wild, and this may be done by enclosing with wire netting as large a portion of ground as can be managed, and providing them with an artificial earth, with a box for a sleeping room, and fresh water to drink. One of the healthiest lot of cubs the writer ever saw had an enclosure made for them in a park, surrounding a clump of larches, underneath which was a patch of high nettles, and where already a colony of rabbits had made their burrows. The cubs promptly took possession of one or two of the largest burrows, but what became of the original inhabitants was a mystery that no one attempted to solve ! The cubs were as wild as if they belonged naturally to the place, and on the approach of any person they at once dived into their rabbit holes in the most approved manner. When they were big enough a small portion of wire was raised up, and the larch-clump being close to a covert the cubs used to go there to forage, and return again to their enclosure during the day-time. After a while the wire netting was removed altogether, and the cubs were left to their own devices. The wire netting should be about six feet high, for if there is a vixen with cubs about she will kill the others if she can get at them.

Q. What food would such cubs be able to catch for themselves ?

A. Chiefly field mice, very small rabbits or rats, young thrushes and blackbirds, and quantities of beetles. It would be a considerable time before they could interfere with winged game, especially wild partridges and pheasants, which would nearly always have a parent bird at hand to warn the young ones. By the time the cubs became old enough to be dangerous foes, the young birds should be pretty well able to take care of themselves.

Q. Would cubs thus brought up be able to show any sport in the following season ?

A. No, very little, for they have had no old vixen to take them about, and teach them the country. Good sport entirely depends on there being a large supply of old foxes ; and it is a mere mockery for an estate owner to make a pretence of providing foxes, and then to show nothing but cubs. Merely to have a fox found is but a small part of the proceeding, the real test being whether a good run has followed.

CHAPTER VI

HARES

ONE of the great advantages of hare-hunting is that it can be carried on in a very unpretentious way, and at little cost, and no extensive tract of country is required in order to enjoy a great deal of real sport. A hare is remarkably cunning, almost more so than a fox, and is even a greater test of a huntsman's skill if it has fair play and is not raced to death by fast hounds, as is too much the fashion of the present day. Small foxhounds go too fast to give a hare a chance of employing all its wiles ; and as the tendency of a hare is nearly always to come round in a circle, there is not the same inducement to hard riders to demand pace, with the object of cutting down the field, when the odds are that before long the last will have become first through no skill of their own, but rather by the force of circumstances. With harriers the chief object should be real " hunting " in contrast to " riding," and enjoyment sought in watching the hounds puzzle out the doubles and various shifts of the hare, more than in galloping and jumping fences.

The style of hunting should be quite different from that of a fox, for with the latter when a

check occurs the probability is that the fox is
still travelling on, though diverted from the course
he was pursuing, and if time is lost in hitting off
the line, the scent will become stale ; a hare, on
the contrary, is almost sure to be lying down
in the immediate vicinity, and therefore it is
necessary to search every likely place very closely
in order to restart the quarry, and to persevere
on the scent, however weak it may be—at any
moment the hunted animal may jump up, and
the hounds get away close behind on a fresh
and capital scent. Patience is, therefore, a great
attribute for a harrier-huntsman ; while the
quickness absolutely essential for a huntsman
of foxhounds is of nothing like such importance
when hunting a hare. In one respect, however,
the talents of a huntsman in either pursuit can
be confidently gauged ; the first-rate man will
frequently kill either fox or hare in out-of-the-
way hiding-places, in farm-buildings, a cart-
shed, barns, poultry-houses, on the roof of a
house, on the top of a wall, ensconced in ivy,
and many other such places of refuge ; while
the man without genius has little success in this
direction, and only manages to catch the animal
he is hunting in a plain, simple way. To him
the wiles of his quarry remain a sealed book, and
the amount of foxes supposed to be " run to
ground," will be quite out of proportion to those
that are killed after a run. Sometimes the advent
of a new huntsman appears to coincide in an
extraordinary way with the predilection of
the pursued to hide themselves in quaint
refuges, which they have not hitherto been
suspected of doing ; and with the departure of
the same huntsman, the fancy for these places

seems no longer to exist. The old proverb may then be aptly quoted that " he who runs may read," and due merit be given to the huntsman who outwits his quarry instead of *vice versâ.* Perhaps no higher meed of praise can be given to any one than for it to be said of him : "He is always killing in a cart-shed ! " It is the best proof possible that he knows his business.

With some huntsmen the sole aim seems to be to have a gallop, and a satisfactory finish to the run appears quite immaterial, so long as they can speedily find another animal to hunt. To them a gentle reminder may be offered, that the object of hunting is to catch your game ; and that anything short of that must be dubbed a failure. Others, on the contrary, seek by any means to attain a kill, and spoil many a promising gallop by using unwarrantable means to drive the quarry into the mouths of the hounds. A huntsman should beware of becoming too bloodthirsty, and should remember that kills without a run are distasteful to his followers ; and that the number of noses on a kennel door do not always signify there has been real sport. " In medio tutissimus ibis " is as safe a maxim to follow as it was in the days of Imperial Rome, and the huntsman who can show a record of excellent gallops, followed by kills in the open, has no need to fear that his light will ever be hid under a bushel.

Many ladies have carried the horn in the wake of harriers with more or less success, and where fields are small, and composed almost entirely of friends and dependants, no possible objection can be urged, especially when the pack is a semi-private one, and there is a capable substitute available to take command whenever needed. Few ladies enjoy such robust health that they can defy the weather, and fatigue inseparable from long days, for any length of time with impunity, though their spirit may carry them seemingly through for the time being. Sometimes the family doctor can tell a different tale, with a grave face and a shake of the head! At any rate, it seems scarcely probable that ladies will be extensively employed as professional huntsmen, and Girton graduates will hardly be able to look forward to such a post as a due reward for their arduous educational efforts!

What is the most suitable standard of height for harriers is ever a burning and much discussed question. From the diminutive rabbit beagle, that can scarcely tire a hare before it has tired itself, and could not hold a full-grown hare if it should chance to get hold of it, to the stately Kerry " beagle," beloved of O'Connell " the Liberator," each has its supporters and earnest advocates. The true harrier, the old-fashioned, serviceable, blue mottled, or black and tan hound is almost improved out of existence, but he had a marvellous tender nose, with indefatigable patience, and was admirably adapted for the work he had to do. The scent of a hare is much weaker than that of a fox, and a foxhound is apt to have too much drive for working out the intricacies of the puzzle set by a crafty old hare, though his speed may enable him to race it down, without giving it the opportunity of putting its wiles in force. This, however, is rather begging the question, and by so doing the essential spirit of hare-hunting is altogether lost. One of the causes of this change of fashion is the desire of winning prizes on the show bench, and hence a good-looking hound is not only kept on account of the impression he makes on the flags, but for the same reason he is actually bred from to the detriment of the pack, when formerly he would have been speedily drafted ruthlessly out of the kennel. Handsome is that handsome does, however, and when it comes to close hunting our handsome friend has frequently to take a back seat at the performance, while some plain, unpretentious hound usurps his place, and reaps a rich reward in the estimation of his huntsman.

Q. What may be considered a useful height for hare-hunting hounds ?

A. This depends very much upon the country, and what is required of them, but they should be fast enough to run a hare down in reasonable time, and able to get quickly over such obstacles as they may meet. A pack that is to be hunted on foot should hardly be so fast as when hunted from horseback ; but if they will meet with high stone walls, or broad ditches, the hounds should be altogether on a larger scale than in an open down country. About eighteen inches used to be considered the height to aim at for harriers, and fifteen inches for foot-beagles, and with a little give and take on either side of these dimensions an extremely useful pack can be formed. Some harrier packs contain hounds that would be no discredit, in the matter of height, to a pack of staghounds, but a hare seems sadly over-matched when pursued by such giants as these !

Though it is needful to keep in mind that it is

the hounds who have to catch the game, and not the huntsman, it is not judicious to overdo a part and have them too large.

Q. Do hares breed more than once a year ?
A. A doe hare breeds probably three or four times in the twelve months.

Q. Do hares pair as rabbits do ?
A· No ; they have broad views as to matrimonial ties !

Q. How many leverets are there usually at a birth ?
A. Generally two, but sometimes three, and very occasionally four or five.

Q. What situations are favourites with hares for making their forms ?
A. Hares will remain in woods and plantations until the leaves fall, when they usually desert them for a time, for the continual falling of leaves seems to " get on their nerves " and annoy them ; and so also do the restless habits of rabbits, and where these are plentiful hares, as a rule, will not stop. They are very sensitive to changes of weather, and as each hare usually has three or four forms in different places, an observant person who gets to know the habits of a particular hare can sometimes make a shrewd guess at an imminent change, according to which form the hare selects for the day. They love to lie warm and dry, and well-sheltered from the prevailing wind. In the winter months, after the turnips have been gathered into pies, rough meadow-fields are a sure find for a hare ; and in fine weather they will lie in a fallow-field that has been ploughed some time, and here they are sure

to be lying within handy distance of a furrow, down which they will run when danger threatens. Where enclosures are small they frequently lie within thirty yards of the fence, through which they can easily pop to make their escape in time of need.   As the wheat grows in the spring and gets high enough to hide them when lying close, it becomes a favourite retreat, for quiet is to be obtained there with plenty of delicious, tender food close at hand.   A swampy spot is almost sure to contain a hare at that time of year, but it is certain to be a doe expecting a family, for she goes there to obtain coolness from the moist ground, which appears to be very grateful to her at that time.

Q.   Can the sexes be distinguished by the appearance of a hare in its form ?

A.   A doe hare usually lies with its ears more drooping on each side than a jack, whose ears are kept closer together on the nape of its neck.

Q.   Is anything to be learned from the carriage of the ears when running ?

A.   If a hare on being roused carries both ears straight up, pointing forward, it is sure to be a strong, stout hare, and may give a long run before it gets beaten.   One that has one ear pointing forward and the other back, and possibly keeps moving the latter up and down, is seldom a hare that will travel far away, though it may prove a very cunning one, and compel a huntsman to use all his craft before the hare is lying at his feet.   A hare that lays both its ears flat on its back, and races off as fast as ever it can go, though the hounds may be some distance behind, is of a timorous disposition, and will probably prove neither stout, nor wily ; but of course there are no hard and fast rules, and much depends upon the circumstances at the time.

Q. Does the quality of the food affect the endurance of hares ?

A. Undoubtedly it does, and when hares are constantly feeding on luscious grass or clover they cannot run as well as when the same is drier, with less sap in it. This may be looked for with the approach of autumn, especially after the occurrence of a few frosty nights, which check the growth of the grass, and send the sap back to the roots. Hares, it may be noted, seldom touch turnips if they have plenty of other food, until winter arrives, and keen frosts set in.

Q. Do any harrier packs wear other colour than green as a hunt uniform ?

A. Scarlet is also very occasionally worn, notably by the Craven Harriers, no foxhounds hunting that district.

With reference to the sport to be obtained with harriers, no doubt an open country is much to be desired, and the wilder the country the better, though first-rate runs are often obtained where the conditions are exactly the opposite. A letter from Mr. Elsey gives such a vivid account of hare-hunting on the Lincolnshire wolds that I am glad to record it as typical of the sport in general, and more especially of that part in particular :—

" For the last two seasons my brother Will has kept a pack of beagles, medium size, and rare sport indeed we have had with them ; my nephew Charlie hunts them on foot.

" The beagles seem generally able to run well ;

and very often can run hard, when I hear afterwards the foxhounds have not been able to run a yard on the same day. A hare—at least one of our high-country hares—takes a lot of killing, so much happens in the run to help the hunted hare : fresh hares or rabbits jumping up ; meeting with the line of a disturbed fox ; the hare running down the hard road, and then crossing and recrossing its own foiled ground or the stale line of others ; in fact a high-country hare takes an immense deal of killing after January comes in.

" Their habits when hunted are very curious. The run hare generally returns to where she was found some time during the run, but a good old hare, after returning, will go the same round again, or take quite an opposite course, even crossing small rivers and swimming drains ; I have seen several hares swim a drain when hard pressed. Really a hare stands a great chance of beating a pack of beagles in our country, but we managed to kill several hares last season after very fine, long runs, seldom getting on killing terms with them under an hour, and generally taking two hours. Twice last season I have tired an old hunter in good condition till he could only raise a trot. You can give a horse a good tiring in a day's beagling.

" I have noticed how hares leave a different scent behind them, and how when the hounds could only run moderately after one hare, with the next one they can run like steam. If it is a hard job to tell a run fox, and requires a good man to do so, it takes a very good man to distinguish a run hare for certain, if two or three others are about. That sometimes happens to us, especially if we have crossed the River Bain, but twice we have got over the difficulty and killed. On the last occasion I spotted a hare in her form, rode close past her, and then, fetching the beagles, told the huntsman the hare had a white star on its forehead, and two very large white streaks below the ears. We ran for two hours and ten minutes, and though the huntsman had laughed when I told him about the streaks, he held her up when we killed, and said, 'You were perfectly right. This is the hare we started with, for here are the marks right enough.' The hounds had kept well to the line, though other hares had several times crossed it; and I now have got the stuffed head at home."

CHAPTER VII

HOUNDS

THE origin of the hound is so ancient that it is quite lost in the mists of antiquity, but the foxhound as we know him to-day is undoubtedly a modern product. The hounds that the Normans hunted with were probably of the type of the St. Hubert breed, and these were gradually improved by selection until the elegant muscular hound of to-day was evolved, a marvel of strength, symmetry, and endurance. What the hounds were like in the Tudor and Stuart periods can scarcely be determined, for, judging from the pictures of their horses, if any likenesses are extant of their hounds they must be very far from being true to nature. During George III.'s reign, however, many portraits were limned of famous hounds which would compare favourably with the winners at a modern Peterborough Show, though no doubt the rank and file of that day were far behind our present packs as far as symmetry and good looks are concerned. Even forty years ago, hounds could be found in most of the fashionable kennels that would not be put forward by many an unpretentious kennel to-day when the puppies are being drafted ; and " John Warde's neckcloth " was then to be seen in every pack, however smart.

Whether our hounds of to-day have as good noses as their predecessors is an oft-discussed question, but though good looks are possibly made more a point of than formerly, it is probably the case that the nose in most cases is there, if only the hound has the opportunity frequently accorded him of perfecting himself in using it. The life of a foxhound is now most artificial from the time he enters the kennel, and except when he is actually out hunting all chance of employing his nose is denied in an ordinary way. How few opportunities he gets a moment's reflection will show. Taking one season with another let us suppose a pack, hunting two days in the week, including cub-hunting, is out fifty times ; then, if the hound is lucky enough to be out every time, steering clear of all accidents and ailments, he gets only fifty opportunities in the year of educating his nose, while we all know what a long time it usually takes our own pets, whether pointer, setter, spaniel, retriever, or terrier, before the young dog can find, and hold, a scent of game like the cunning old hero of many seasons. And yet our young dog probably is taken out for a run amongst game every day of the year—if, indeed, he is not constantly running about loose—and consequently gets as many opportunities of snuffing about, and learning to use his nose, as there are days in the year. In all probability the ancient hounds had much more freedom than the present ones have, and were treated more like trencher-fed hounds, and if so their noses would be bound to serve the puppies better than would those of hounds closely confined in kennels, except when at exercise under careful supervision. A young dog of any breed who can at once successfully eclipse his practised comrade on a weak scent is as rarely found as an infant prodigy !

Tales that have come down from our grandfathers of marvels that bloodhounds have shown, and that have usually been looked upon as having grown with the efflux of time, do not now seem so incredible when judged by some of the performances of bloodhounds, tested with "the clean boot," at recent trials.

If foxhounds possess the same olfactory powers the wonder is that a fox should ever be lost ! Certainly some of the hounds hunting rough moorland countries, where hounds are necessarily very frequently left entirely to themselves, and are often trencher-fed, develop a keenness of nose and a gift of tongue not always to be found in the more fashionable packs. That a late Duke of Grafton thoroughly believed this he showed in a practical way when, in 1862, he purchased from the late Mr. John Hill the pack with which he had hunted the moorland country between Thornton dale and Scarborough.

It is a common belief that the very broad muzzle and nostrils of the bloodhound are the cause of its low-scenting powers, and to a certain extent this is very likely right ; but it must not be overlooked that animals with very pointed muzzles,—witness the fox, for instance—often are gifted with very keen scent, and therefore the breadth of muzzle has probably very little to do with it. Points that were frequently pressed upon me in my boyhood by a famous breaker of pointers and setters, William Thursby, were that no dog had first-rate scenting powers unless it was long in the muzzle, and also had the wings of the nostrils largely developed, thus enabling the dog to open its nostrils very wide, to catch the faintest taint of scent on the breeze. In both respects after-experience has seemed to prove that the observant old man was perfectly right, and that these points, rather than mere breadth, were the essential ones required.

In furtherance of this view attention may be called to the Podencos of Spain and Portugal, which, though they resemble somewhat a prick-eared lurcher in appearance, pack together like hounds, and appear able to hunt the faintest scent, on ground baked by a southern sun. Years ago when at Jerez de la Frontera in Spain, the late Mr. Henry Davies, who then had the chief management of a pack of English harriers that hunted the district, mentioned to me that they hardly ever killed a hare without being helped by a Podenco joining in the hunt, and assisting them when they were run out of scent. It is an interesting fact that, in a very early picture by De Bridt of hawking in the seventeenth century that till lately hung at Kirby Hall, there is an excellent portrait of a Podenco. There is also a likeness of a Blenheim spaniel, not the snub-nosed dog seen at a modern dog-show, but with a muzzle similar to any working spaniel of Devonshire or Cornwall of the present time.

Regarding hounds of the black St. Hubert breed, these were bloodhounds, and unless the Kerry Beagles can trace their descent from them, the only pack known to the writer was that belonging to the late Mr. Neville, of Chilland, near Winchester, who was accustomed to hunt tame stags with them, but often also used them as harriers. Though unfortunately deformed at birth, Mr. Neville contrived to hunt under grave difficulties, and had a marvellous command over animals, to every species of which he was devotedly attached. He may not always have been strictly orthodox in the management of his pack, but there was always an undercurrent of common sense in all that he did; and in giving occasional raw meat to his hounds, which at that time was regarded as the act almost of a madman, he but anticipated the teaching of veterinary science up-to-date in the treatment of eczema. Those who were privileged to hunt with him will remember how a certain deer used to live in the same paddock with the hounds; and how, after giving a good run, the stag would trot amicably home in the middle of the pack, not far from Mr. Neville's stirrup-leather. The numerous schoolgirls and lady-telegraph-clerks who signed the notorious petition against the Royal Buckhounds might well consider this aspect of the case! A picture in oils of the above "Return from the Chase," of which Mr. Neville was very proud, used to hang in his dining-room. At another period he had a tame jackal, which was accustomed to lie on the hearthrug in front of the drawing-room fire, and go out exercising with the pack, yet they ran it with zest when its turn came to give a run, on which occasion the jackal invariably made straight for home, no matter where it was turned out.

Mr. Neville more than once told me how he

became possessed of those hounds. From time immemorial each keeper in the New Forest had been required to keep one of these St. Hubert's, to aid in tracking deer-stealers, and also for following wounded deer; but an edict went forth in the middle of the last century that the hounds were to be done away with, whereupon Mr. Neville secured the nucleus of his pack. He believed that the original hounds came from Germany, far away in the Middle Ages. The pack was eventually purchased by the late Lord Roden, and they afterwards became the property of Lord Wolverton.

From the diminutive rabbit beagle to the stately staghound all are true hounds, that is they differ from other members of the canine race who pursue their game by scent, in that they hunt together in a pack, instead of each working for itself alone. This is the great distinguishing characteristic of hounds, marking them out from all others, who, though they may join together for a few moments, do so to benefit themselves, and not to work together as a body corporate. But hounds, on the contrary, are thorough exponents of the ideals of Socialism! Two maxims that go far towards making a hunting pack of hounds should be learned by heart and ever kept in mind—" Good looks and perfection in form are of no use without nose," and " A hound that picks up a scent, and does not at once throw his tongue to inform his comrades of the fact that they may come and assist him, should have no place in a pack of hounds."

To the following questions Tom Smith, the huntsman of the Bramham Moor hounds, has kindly furnished the answers:—

Q. What standard of height do you recommend for dogs and bitches ?

A. "For dogs, 23½ inches.
For bitches, 22½ inches."

Q. What are the chief points to be looked for ?

A. "Good necks and shoulders are most necessary, with good arched ribs, straight legs, good feet, loins, and quarters."

Q. Is the idea correct that throaty hounds are very low-scented ?

A. "No, and the appearance is not good. Throaty hounds are usually slow."

Q. Are hare-footed hounds generally good travellers ; and keep their toes up better than round-footed ones ? Or is the reverse the case ?

A. "The reverse is the case. It is also against their appearance on the flags."

Q. Are you in favour of now unusual colours, such as pure white ; lemon-pie ; hare-pie ; badger-pie ; all black ; or black and white hounds ?

A. "No. Bad-coloured hounds are quite out of date. Nothing is so fashionable at present as the Belvoir tan.

"I don't condemn bad-coloured hounds on any other grounds except for appearance. I have known some most excellent hounds in work, and clever-shaped as well, of various colours, but you must go with the fashion, and nowadays people will not breed from bad-coloured hounds, and scarcely look at them. The Duke of Beaufort's used to be nearly all badger-pied, but now they are chiefly marked with black, tan, and white. Where you have the advantage of breeding a lot of puppies, of course all the bad-coloured ones are put away when whelped. A nice whole-coloured pack is more taking to the eye, both in the kennel and in the field, than one with some odd-coloured ones in it, and nearly all countries go for that at the present day."

Q. What is the most effective number of hounds for a pack to take into the field?

A. "An average pack is about twenty-five couple, but it depends upon the country that is to be hunted."

Q. How many should be calculated per day's hunting, to commence the season with?

A. "For four days a week fifty couple, to allow for brood bitches."

Q. How many hours' exercise should hounds get before cub-hunting begins?

A. "Begin with one hour, and gradually work on to six hours, on three days in the week."

Q. How many weeks beforehand should the long exercise commence?

A. "A month."

Q. Do you recommend rounding hounds, considering all things?

A. "Yes. Firstly, it adds to their appearance. Secondly, it helps them through distemper.

Q. How often should hounds be "dressed" during the summer? Can you recommend any particular application?

A. "Once a year, about the time the young hounds are rounded. There are various good applications."

Q. What treatment should hounds receive on coming in from hunting?

A. "They should be fed, and then be moved

out for a few minutes ; after which get them at
once upon their beds, first removing any thorns
that have been picked up. By no means have
them washed."

Q. How should puppies be dealt with on
coming in from walk ?
A. " They should have a little cooling
medicine occasionally, and as much grass-yard
exercise as possible."

Q. What treatment do you recommend for
distemper ?
A. " There are various receipts for this.
Plenty of fresh air and good nursing are most
necessary."

Q. What is the best site for kennels ?
A. " A south aspect, on rising ground if
possible, and plenty of water."

Q. What soil is most suitable ?
A. " Gravel should be selected if possible."

Q. What causes kennel lameness ?
A. " Kennel idleness in many instances,
through being left in the kennel too much, and
not enough out in the fresh air."

Q. What is a good material for floors ? Should
sawdust be used in sleeping-rooms ?
A. " The floors of the lodging-rooms should
consist of two yards of concrete and cement, with
a good fall from each side to a channel in the
centre. Sawdust should not be used in the
sleeping-rooms, only bracken or straw."

Q. How high and wide should the benches
be ?
A. " The benches should be wooden, with

latted bottoms, about a foot from the floor. They should be about two yards square. I quite endorse the opinion of the huntsman you speak about, that many quarrels are started by benches being too wide ; and not only that, it tempts them to stale and empty themselves on their beds."

(The opinion referred to was that many quarrels begin, when wide benches are used, from a hound in the back row stepping over his tired comrades in front, when he wants to go outside for any purpose, and such unwarranted familiarity is strongly objected to.)

Q. Please state a suitable length and width for troughs.

A. "Troughs should be on wheels, about five yards in length. In width they should be about a foot at the bottom to a foot-and-a-half at the top, and a foot-and-a-half in depth."

Q. If hounds are quarrelling at night, is it safe to go into them without wearing kennel clothes, and taking a whip ?

A. " Certainly not."

With reference to the necessity for these precautions it should be remembered that hounds are very powerful animals, and often savage when their passions have been raised by fighting. The mere use of the voice is not sufficient to control them at night, on such occasions, without the outward symbols of authority which they are accustomed to obey, and which they at once recognise, and acknowledge accordingly. Serious injuries have sometimes been suffered through going into the kennel at such times in ordinary clothes, when the inmates have failed to recognise the person endeavouring to quell the riot, and a fatal termination is not unknown.

Q. Have you any remarks to make about "master" hounds? Do hounds usually select a particular place, and always lie there?

A. "Some hounds are more quarrelsome in the kennel than others, and you find this runs in certain strains; and of course more so in the summer when not doing much work. You will often find a hound more quarrelsome than the rest fare the worst, for the others take a dislike to him.

" I don't think hounds occupy certain positions on their benches, but lie anywhere."

Q. With regard to food, how old should the oatmeal be? Can a rough estimate be given as to the quantity required for a specified time?

A. "If you have the accommodation, have the meal in the bins twelve months before using it. About twenty to twenty-five tons is required per year for fifty couple of hounds."

Q. Should any other kind of meal be mixed with oatmeal, for a change?

A. "No. Nothing beats pure oatmeal."

Q. Can you give any hints about the broth, and flesh for the hounds?

A. "The flesh should be well boiled and well chopped. A medium quantity should be mixed in their feed, with half broth and half water, regulated according to the work the hounds are doing."

Q. How is water best supplied?

A. " The water for feeding should be boiled."

Q. What remarks have you to make about suitable medicines ? Should sulphur be given periodically ?

A. " An occasional dose of Epsom salts does hounds good ; and a little sulphur mixed in their food now and again is beneficial."

Q. What are the ordinary hours for feeding in summer, and winter ? What are the ordinary hours for feeding before hunting ? What are the ordinary hours for feeding delicate hounds ?

A. " In the summer-time the best time to feed is about four o'clock in the afternoon, and in the winter about eight o'clock in the morning. The pack intended for hunting should not be fed after the previous morning, but have a good feed after returning from hunting. Delicate hounds require a bit twice a day, especially after a hard day."

Q. Do you find certain traits run in families such as road-hunting ; extra drive ; good drawers in covert, &c. ?

A. " Certainly, and it requires a lot of studying in breeding hounds, to mate them so as to nick in with the different qualities."

In illustration of this in the early sixties a hound, Layman, in the York and Ainsty pack, had the habit of always seizing the fox's head, when one was killed, and either carrying it till another fox was found, or else taking it home to the kennels—for at that time it was not the custom to attach the fox's mask to the whip's saddle ; Layman continued this practice until a son of his, Villager, a very fine hound, was admitted into the pack, and the latter, being possessed of no filial respect, proceeded to usurp his sire's prerogative, and ever afterwards carried the head himself.

10

As to the pace of hounds, whether in the present day this has been somewhat sacrificed to scenting qualities or not, opinions differ even amongst experts, but so long as a fox is fairly chased by scent, and not by sight, it seems difficult to say that hounds can be too fast, for, after all, it must be the nose that directs the legs. In the case of a view it is different, and the faster hounds are bred the more chance there must be of chopping a fox the moment he is roused, before he has had time to get fairly on his legs ; but for every other reason it would seem the faster hounds can go the more use they will make of the scent, and keep nearer to the fox ; and this again results in a better scent, through it not having time to become dissipated in the air before the hounds can pick it up.

In the remarks previously made about harriers, however, it was there explained that it is not advisable to have very speedy hounds to hunt hares, as there is much more pleasure to be derived from the wiles of a hare, and unravelling them, than in simply racing a weak animal to death.

The two views of the case have been ably put forward by Mr. Elsey and Tom Smith, and after perusing them it is hoped that each person will feel able to decide the case for himself, to his own satisfaction.

The former writes as follows :—

" I think hounds have been bred so much for pace and looks, and so fast, that many and many a run has ended in failure that probably should have been a good one. The fox has been obliged to turn short, and either return to covert or else run very cunning, or if he does keep straight

and there is a scent he pays the penalty after a
quick but short burst. They have now got
hounds so quick and handy, and so are the
huntsman and whips, that a fox has no chance of
getting the start he requires, and which in fair
play he should be allowed to have.

" People will tell you that you should get away
with the hounds on the top of the fox. I say,
breed hounds with nose and music. They would
then hunt a fox really well, and drive him if there
was a scent, and with luck end in a kill after a
good hunt, which would well satisfy all except a
few hard thrusters. As for the thrusters, I don't
suppose they ever were satisfied ; in fact foxes are
not fast or strong enough to do so without losing
their lives. The pace of hounds has been immensely improved, and also the pace of the
horses, but it has been forgotten to consider
whether foxes could stand this extra pace, for it
is, I believe, certain that they have not been
improved in the same degree."

And now let us hear the other side of the question, from Tom Smith :—

" Mr. Elsey remarks hounds have been bred too
fast, but I don't think so, at least for the requirements of the present day, for in the shires, and
even in this country, with the enormous fields
that come out hunting hounds must have pace,
and plenty of drive, to keep out of the way of the
riders, and a good fox with anything like luck,
even with a good scent, will generally manage to
stand up before hounds for fifty minutes or more.

" My opinion about short-running foxes is, that
since shooting has come to the pitch it has now,
and so many tame pheasants are reared, the old
foxes are done away with, and the cubs hand-

reared. These, of course, do not get to know the country till they are a couple of years old, if indeed they are lucky enough to live so long, for the life of a cub deprived of the guidance of its parents must be very precarious, what with keepers and other mischances, besides its own legitimate foes, a pack of foxhounds."

It may help to reconcile these two opinions by considering the respective countries in which each hunts, the one where very small fields are the rule, while game preserving is by no means overdone, and every one almost welcomes a fox ; while in the other country game preserving on a large scale is rife, and the fields that come out hunting are enormous. The governing conditions in the two countries are therefore considerably different.

As to the pace some foxhounds possess, I was once witness of an extraordinary performance by a young hound in the Bedale pack. We were drawing Hutton Moor, not far from Ripon, when a fox jumped up in view, and Singer raced out from the rest of the pack, caught the fox after one or two turns, and killed it. Very shortly after, another fox was roused not far from the high ragged fence skirting the moor, and through this hedge the fox quickly slipped. Again Singer raced after it, and though it had got a long start the enclosure adjoining happened to be a very large grass-field, and before the fox could reach the further hedge Singer rolled it over, and killed it also. Later in the day we had about an hour's run, when in crossing a park the fox was viewed, and again leaving the pack well behind Singer shot out, and killed his third fox that day. Almost as remarkable as his speed was the young hound's courage, for there are not many which will tackle a fox single-handed, and kill it.

Singer was walked by the late Mr. W. Tappin, of Nunwick, and his son, Mr. Tappin, of Claro Bank House, Ripon, some years ago kindly sent me the pedigree of the hound, written by an old member of the Bedale Hunt, who knew him from his birth.

" Singer entered in 1870, was walked by the late Mr. Tappin at Nunwick, and got his speed from chasing the hares, many of which he ran down in the pastures by the riverside. As to his courage with a fox, on the principle that familiarity breeds contempt, he has often as a pup been seen playing with fox-cubs bred in the Willow Garth Wood near his home, which wood was the most certain find for a fox during the mastership of Mr. Booth.

" Singer never showed great speed after his first year when he ran from sight ; and when he got settled down to run from nose, he was no longer conspicuous for speed. He remained in the pack till seven years old."

		Bramham Moor.	Belvoir.	
Singer ent. 1870	{	Stormer out of Charity	{ Stormer Royalty } Clinker	
			{ Cromwell—Chorister—Contest* Toilet	

Mr. Tappin also remarks :—

" The dog and I have spent many happy hours with the old hares when I was a boy, and he was being walked, and no doubt it was his early running after these hares that gave him such a good turn of speed afterwards.

* Lord H. Bentinck's.

CHAPTER VIII

HUNTERS

To completely enjoy a day's hunting it is necessary that the horse that carries you should not only be a pleasant animal to ride, but should also thoroughly understand the fences he is likely to encounter, for the ordinary individual hunts for pleasure, and not to break horses. Yet looking back over nearly fifty years of following the chase, and all the great horses I have been fortunate enough to ride during that long period, in many different countries—horses that could gallop and jump, and follow close to hounds however far and fast they ran—there have been very few indeed that were easy ones to ride—anybody's horse, in fact—and almost every one has had its own peculiar idiosyncrasies. Those that have been very gentle and amiable have usually been of little account, while the capable, stout-hearted animals have been more or less a handful to ride, especially when they were fresh at starting. Of the multitude of horses that are brought into the hunting-field, very few, comparatively, possess the gift of going, sufficient to satisfy the aspirations of the ardent spirit whose sole thought is " to be with them I

will "; and when in addition to great capabilities
a horse has the manners of a lady's park-hack,
the purse-strings should be loosened, and the
animal secured at any price, if there is a sufficient
balance at the bank to allow the extravagance,
for verily such horses will be seldom met with
throughout the experience of a long life.

While an animal may be a perfect hunter in
one kind of country, he may be a very different
one, even an unsafe conveyance, in another where
the fences are of quite an altered character. The
high-spirited, galloping horse, which may be
invaluable amongst the oxers round the famous
covert, " John o'Gaunt," might easily break his
own neck, and his rider's too, over the huge
banks in Cornwall, if he had not had any
previous schooling over such obstacles, and
came fresh to them from a flying country—
such banks, for instance, as those near Padstow,
which are faced with limestone slates, set on
edge in herring-bone fashion, and which can
gash a horse like a knife, if he is so unfortunate
as to hit them with his knees or hind fetlocks.
On the other hand, a steed that might be perfect
over such banks, which would bound to the top
of one seven or eight feet high, and then, if
necessary, walk along it, or turn round and come
back the same way it went up, might yet be
dangerous at timber if taken to the shires, might
utterly decline to face a thick bulfinch, or tumble
ignominiously with its rider into the first brook
he came across, when it first made the acquaintance of such unaccustomed fences.

Experience, then, has taught one that horses
from a purely banking country, unused to thorn
fences, are often a long time before they learn

that strong ones must be treated with respect, and cannot be rushed through without a fall; and they are likewise frequently contemptuous of timber. A horse, however, who has been reared amongst thorn fences, will usually take to banks, if he is quiet and sensible, and is generally a better wall-jumper than even those to which they are native, for he is not so apt to knock off the top stones when he jumps, from simple carelessness. One thing, however, may be laid down as an axiom—a mad, hot-headed brute is no "hunter" in any country; and I quite agree with a favourite saying of the late Mr. George Lane-Fox, the famous Master of the Bramham Moor, that "no horse is a hunter until he will *walk* through a gap." A great deal of shrewd observation and common sense underlies that remark.

It follows, therefore, from the dissimilarity of different hunting countries, that ideas vary almost as much as to the type of horse that should be considered perfect for a hunter. Hence also arise many letters to the press laying down such contrary rules as to the royal road to breed one. The man who lives all his life in a wild hill-country wants a stiff-made, short-legged, powerful horse, not more than fifteen one, or fifteen two, as he often has to dismount and lead him up or down steep places; and he has no objection to a dash of pony blood in his steed, while pace is not so much the consideration as sagacity, docility, surefootedness, and ability to stand great fatigue and very long days. The fortunate possessor of a large stud in the Midlands requires quite a different animal. His notion is probably that a hunter should be sixteen one or two hands high, able to gallop at a great pace, and to jump high and wide. A sticky horse, that might be excellent among the hills, would be an abomination in Leicestershire, where, so long as he covers plenty of ground in his leaps and gets up high enough to clear the fences, it does not greatly matter whether he misjudges the distance a little, and takes off a foot or two too soon. A horse that would be an unpleasant, even a dangerous, mount in some countries may be a perfect one elsewhere, and when big flying fences have to be encountered plenty of dash and courage are required to surmount them in safety.

A sticky horse that must stop and look before it leaps is quite useless in the Midlands for a hard rider, for many of the fences there met with would be quite impassable barriers to such a steed, and the man who rode it would perforce be obliged to perform the *rôle* of a looker-on whether he wished it or not. It would be absolutely impossible for him to take a place amongst the gallant leaders, who cut out the work at the tail of the flying pack. Yet that very horse in a totally different country might be a real treasure to an ambitious rider who wanted to keep with hounds in a rough, intricate district, where a careful, clever horse is the first necessity, and where a dashing animal might soon land its rider in difficulties the more sober-minded steed would be sure to avoid.

For three years the writer hunted an animal with a good deal of Arabian blood in it, which was the very best horse he ever rode amongst moorlands, able to gallop its best pace over the heather without putting a foot wrong ; that

would race down steep hill-sides without a
stumble, or gallop up them without ever a sob;
and yet proved perfectly useless on a change
of residence into a lowland country, for nothing
would induce the horse to jump a fence except
at a stand; and at last it was obliged to be sold
out of the stud in consequence. It was one of
the frequent instances of qualities not proving
hereditary, for the dam had been an excellent
hunter, while the sire was Duc de Beaufort, a
winner, amongst other races, of the Sefton
Steeplechase at Liverpool.

Another instance of a horse proving brilliant
in one country, though useless in another, is that
of Lackland, by King John out of Gaiety by
Touchstone, bred by the late Mr. Blenkiron at
the Middle Park stud. He won ten races on the
flat in England, one of them being the Londes-
borough Plate at York, in which the second was
Major Stapylton's famous horse Syrian, who
subsequently ran second for the Cambridgeshire.
After winning the Welter Plate at Pontefract, it
was endeavoured to teach him to jump, but he
had no liking for the job, and it was with the
greatest difficulty he could be induced to get somehow over even a sheep-hurdle. He was so good-
tempered over his difficulties, too, that he would
have made an excellent hunter if only he had
had a natural gift of jumping. I then took him
to Gibraltar, and as hunting was in full swing
when we arrived, I rode him out to see the
hounds at San Roque, not having any other
animal to ride. It so happened we had a fast
gallop, right up to the very foot of the " Queen
of Spain's chair," and Lackland kept close to the
hounds all the way, without making any mistake,

as though he had been to the manner born. Those who know the locality will gladly own this was no mean performance for a horse that had all his life been galloping on the smoothest of turf, and he proved an excellent sure-footed hunter with the Calpe Hounds.

Lackland was a horse of unbounded nerve, as was shown on the day of the inspection of the 2nd Battalion Rifle Brigade by General Somerset, soon after its arrival at Gibraltar, in November, 1874. We were quartered in the Buena Vista Barracks, and when we were drawn up in line for the General Salute the whole of the available space was occupied, there being barely room for me to take my post as adjutant, between the left flank of the regiment and the boundary wall. My horse, too, was almost touching one of the great siege guns, of which two were placed here, overlooking the straits. The boundary wall was very low indeed, and below it the cliff went sheer down to the sea-beach, a very awkward position for any one to be placed in if riding a frightened horse, for the wall was no protection or obstacle to prevent it jumping over to certain death.

Whilst we were forming the parade, a squad of artillerymen, under a subaltern, came up to the gun where I was standing, and proceeded to go through the motions of loading, and I said in joke, " I hope you are not going to fire the gun ! " " Indeed, we are," was the response. Quite horrified, I pointed out that it was impossible that gun-practice should take place during the General's inspection ; but as the officer was im-pervious to argument, I touched Lackland with the spur, and dashed up to the Colonel, in front

of the line. The latter was equally startled as I
was; but before any action could be decided on,
an orderly who had been sent forward to give
notice of the approach of the General, came
running back exclaiming, "Here he is!" and
we had to hurry back to our places.

I had barely got into dressing with the line,
and drawn my sword, when the General appeared,
in front of the Staff, riding through the little
gorge leading on to the ground. As soon as all
were well in view the artillery officer gave the
word of command, and with a deafening roar
that shook every building in the place, and broke
innumerable panes of glass, the big gun was
discharged, and I was enveloped in smoke. The
effect was really ludicrous! Round went the
Staff, round went the General's horse, and away
the terrified horses fled out of the barracks! As
a stage effect it was really perfect. Lackland,
fortunately for me, never flinched at all, or,
blinded as we were by the smoke, we might
easily have gone over the cliff, if he had plunged.
He just gave a tremendous start, and then
standing perfectly still gazed around to see
what was happening. In due time the Staff
reappeared again, and it is needless to say that
no more guns were fired that day, while the
young officer who had caused this contretemps
was given ample opportunities subsequently of
dwelling on the foolishness of playing practical
jokes on elderly general officers on duty. It
appeared, on inquiry, that the colonel com-
manding the artillery had not seen the garrison
orders ordering the inspection, and was unaware
that it was taking place. The artillery and the
infantry were under separate commanders, who

issued their own orders to their men, and though the artillery colonel was under the major-general's command in some things, the arrangements for drill were entirely separate—and in this instance they had clashed, though the subaltern of the artillery was well aware that there was a mistake somewhere, and that it was for him to give way in this case.

Lackland won several races for me in Spain and Portugal, and was eventually sold to go to the stud in the latter country, where the poor little horse came to a disastrous end in the pursuit of his new duties—which was, perhaps, typical of his adopted country! He met with a serious and unique accident, the wound was neglected, inflammation set in, and he succumbed to bad nursing. Poor Lackland, he was a gallant horse!

For hunting in a moorland country no one would dream of giving such a price for even the most perfect animal, as is almost daily given for a good hunter in the shires. The grand criterion of money must, after all, indicate which is accepted as the most perfect type of hunter. It is difficult to combine pace, jumping ability, sense, and weight-carrying power, which are *all* absolutely essential for a Leicestershire horse; and rare articles that many people want are necessarily expensive.

These are the considerations that ought to influence a judge, when making a selection in the show-ring. Other points being equal, he must keep before him which is the animal of the highest value, and make his decision accordingly, irrespective of the particular part of the country in which the show is being held. Men who have never ridden in the shires, and have passed their hunting career amongst small enclosures, do not always attach sufficient importance to the possession of pace, and are apt to be enamoured of a stiffly-built horse, that would be hopelessly tailed off in the first five minutes of a good gallop in the great grazing countries. It is often an uphill task to try to persuade them that their selection may not be the right one, and would probably be well sold at from £90 to £120. Their imagination does not soar to a horse which is *cheap* at £300, and they will overlook such a one in favour of another which resembles something that has carried them in safety over their own sticky country at home.

Their experience being but limited, they are usually the more likely to hold closely to their opinions, and especially is this the case when judging four-year-olds and unbroken young ones. The riders that compose an ordinary field in their own hunt also being usually numbered only by "tens," they do not know what it is to thread a way through the immense crowds that come out in the fashionable countries; and how fast it is often necessary to gallop to catch the rapidly vanishing pack, that literally are racing after the fox when the scent is good. Being accustomed to leisurely proceedings, they do not realise that the steady, good, but slow horse that has carried them safely to their own hounds does not represent the perfection in hunters they have so contentedly imagined it to be. In drawing the inimitable character of Mr. Sawyer on his first visit to the shires, the late Major Whyte-Melville portrayed only too vividly the disillusionment that has been experienced by many another keen rider from the provinces, when he has essayed to ride up to one of the Midland packs on the horses he has been accustomed to go to the front on when hunting at home.

Another cause of difference of opinion as to what a hunter should be, arises from the various motives that urge a man to hunt; and the vast majority of those who compose an ordinary field— in England, at any rate—have no intention of riding close up to the hounds, or running any undue risks whatever. Some come out chiefly to see their friends, and to hear or relate the last good story from town. Others hunt for the sake of health. Many hunt for hunting's sake, but their nervous constitution is such that it gives them no pleasure to ride at big fences, or indeed at any fences at all; and each man carries in his own mind the kind of horse he likes to ride, and persuades himself that this is the proper sort for a hunter. Such a rider, if he is a heavy-weight, is apt to like to bestride an animal as broad in the beam as he is himself; he looks for plenty of bone, and wants to feel something solid under him. He desires plenty of time to collect his thoughts between one fence and another, even if he has only walked through a gap, and is about to go through the next gate, and the pace at which a thoroughbred horse skims over the ground would disconcert him greatly. For him, therefore, a good-shaped steed, not very far removed from an active plough mare on the dam's side, is very likely to be most suitable, and this becomes the proper type in his eyes that a weight-carrier should be. His neighbour, equally heavy, but of a thin, tall, wiry build, means instead to ride his own line, and if hounds run fast to be next to them if he can, and he would consider the last described horse as not a hunter at all, but only fit to take him to the meet in a brougham. The hunter he requires must be a lengthy, far-reaching, big, but short-legged horse, as wiry as himself, and either quite thoroughbred, or so nearly so as to make no practical difference. If these two men meet as judges in a show-ring, each argues from his own standpoint, and how are their ideas to be reconciled? And when each ventilates his opinions in print, how can the public decide between their views, when the merits and the performances of the disputants are quite an unknown quantity, though both are known to be men of experience?

A friend once made a terse remark that nearly hits off the idiosyncrasies of the hunting-field. "Every one," said he, "goes out hunting to get a qualm, but some men require a very big fence before they can experience one; while others get one from a very tiny obstacle indeed! But so long as each gets his qualm he has enjoyed his day, and goes home happy!"

It is with very different views, then, that people congregate at the meet, and it is probably correct to say that more real lovers of hunting, *per se*, are likely to be found at a meet in the so-called provinces than at one in the shires.

In all the main characteristics the conformation of a hunter should be the same wherever he is going to perform, and it is very certain that a really good horse can go in any country, no matter how high bred he may be. It is quite a mistake to imagine a horse must be underbred to creep and crawl in cramped places, for not only can a thoroughbred do the same if he is the right sort, but he probably is also more sensible, and he is certain to be much more active, than his low-bred compeer. The same well-set-on head and neck, sloping shoulders, short, strong back, good quarters, arched ribs, long, powerful forearms, well-developed second thighs, and good legs and feet are required in every country, and in every class of horse, and given these requisites, with a generous, bold, even temperament, the thoroughbred will always out-pace, and out-stay the other. When one hears of riders having to dismount and lead their steeds home after an exceptionally hard day, it is a safe bet to make that they had not been riding thoroughbred horses, if they were in any condition to go at all. I have never owned a thoroughbred horse in my life that would not trot home, though many a time there have been more than twenty miles to cover, after a specially hard day.

To illustrate the above remarks I may mention that some years ago I was riding Belmont, when we were drawing some wild gorse on the steep sides of Knock Ion, a lofty hill on the shores of Lough Derravaragh in Westmeath. Belmont was a beautifully bred horse, by Cambuslang out of Geraldine by Solon (the sire of Barcaldine) out of Gramachree the own sister of Irish Birdcatcher, and Faugh a Ballagh. Belmont had won many races for me, but just then he was crawling about over rocks and hillocks on the mountain sides like any old shooting pony, when a lady rode up to me and said, "Isn't that Belmont? I thought you were going to run him again." "So I am," was the reply. "But what are you going to run him in?" she rejoined; "and why are you

riding him here ? " looking around at the rocks.
" I am not quite sure," I replied, " what I shall
run him in, but I think in the Dunboyne Plate at
Fairyhouse, and the Conyngham Cup at Punchestown." She said no more, but gazed at the horse
as if she was mystified. I did run him for both
the races I had named, in about ten weeks
afterwards, and he won them both.

Mr. Elsey's experience of jumping horses has
been so large that his opinion is most valuable on
the subject, and he has been kind enough to
forward the following remarks :—

" People always did, and always will, vary much
in their opinion of horses. I have had many
good judges over, and learned the fads of many
of them and put them together, which helps
one to know the points of a horse. I think
the best hunter is a 15–3½ or 16 hands, long,
deep-barrelled horse, with short legs, good
shoulders, and strong well-let-down hindquarters,
with a good back, and a good blood head and
neck properly put on, so as to bend nicely to the
bit. He should carry himself well balanced,
with full control of his hind legs, have good large
hocks with plenty of good flat bone below, and
not cut away there at all. His elbows must be at
liberty, and not touch his ribs ; and he must
carry his girths and saddle in the right place.

" The shoulders must be rather strong, long,
and sloping, and well let down at the points. He
must move with good level hunting action, with
his knees showing well in front when you are on
his back, and with full liberty in all his paces.
A horse easy to ride, and easy to guide ; free
from all rush ; and one that you can ask to
steady himself while you take a look at what

is before you without apparently stopping much, and then able to make a big jump, at short notice from your wrist. A fall from a horse made and shaped like this won't hurt you half as much, probably, as one would from a tight-coupled, strong-ribbed, and short-shouldered horse, built like a grindstone, but with a constitution capable of going hunting much oftener than my kind of hunter. The first horse you can ride down to the ground if you fall; with the second you are off before he gets there, with a great chance of breaking your collar-bone.

" Owing to wire, a galloping, hard-pulling, fine-jumping young horse is not suitable for many countries, though such were no pleasure to me to ride at any time. I like a horse to ride that will take a look for himself, with sense enough for both of us. It saves many a fall! One that won't rush, and one that will get well up at his timber when tired. Of course pace comes first. A horse must have pace, and be a fine galloper to be a hunter, and first class.

" Don't pamper them in the stable like hot-house plants. Give them plenty of good food and water, and plenty of exercise, and never allow them to be knocked about or punished. Especially never punish at the wrong moment; and the less punishment the better in most cases. If you fall out with, and punish your horse in the morning, he very often repays you before night.

" I like rye-grass and white clover well har-vested, and having taken just a proper heat in the stack, better than meadow-hay to hunt on— or, for the matter of that, to race on either.

" When seeking to purchase a horse, if I find

a good one I am anxious to buy, I value the 'history' of that horse."

The typical hunter should stand square on his legs, though many a good horse has knees arched, or backward, or hocks bent too much under him. Such malformations may not interfere with his capacity for galloping or jumping, though they throw an undue strain on the limbs, and are a decided eyesore. In a first-rate performer they may be overlooked, provided the **hocks, knees,** sinews, and bone, are exceptionally strong and well developed. But a horse with these blemishes can only be bought by reason of his performances, or by a poor man at a cheap price, and is difficult to sell again if the stud has to be reduced.

Q. What points should be looked for in the head and neck?

A. The eye should be large and generous-looking, not small, "pig-eyed," restless, or sullen. Much of the character of the horse may be gauged by the eye. The outer portion of the eye-ball, the cornea, should not be too convex, and protrude beyond the eyelids, for such animals are frequently short-sighted, and given to shying. This formation is sometimes termed "buck-eye." On looking into the eye with a strong light thrown upon it, and something black and of a dull nature—such as a felt hat—held up in front so as to prevent the light being reflected on the outer surface, search should be made in the interior for cataract, which if present will probably appear as a small white speck, which does not move as the operator continues his investigation. This spot must not be confused with any speck on the cornea (the outer portion of the eyeball), for such would not be the effect of disease probably, might only be temporary, and would only affect the sight by obstructing the light, if in the centre of the cornea; if on one side it will probably be of little importance, unless of considerable size.

A cause of impeded sight is one that is not very common and seldom suspected, and yet might largely diminish the usefulness of a hunter. In the centre of the pupil may be seen a dark body, the corpus nigrum, and sometimes this is so abnormally large that the sight of that eye is completely obscured. This any one can judge for himself, as it is easily seen.

If any doubt exists as to the presence of cataract the horse should be taken into a dark stable, and a light procured (an ordinary match will do) and passed backwards and forwards in front of the suspected eye. If it is healthy three reflections of the light should appear, two being upright, which should follow the movement of the light, and the third inverted, which should move in the contrary direction to the others. If only two reflections are seen the eye is diseased.

The horse should have a long head; be broad between the eyes, with long nostrils when at rest; have good, large ears; and be wide enough between the angle of the jaws to insert between them the outstretched forefinger, including its knuckle.

Q. Why should a horse have a long head ?
A. A short-headed horse, especially a gelding, has nearly always silly ways even if he is not a fool. A horse, too, with a short head has always a short body, for two and a half heads equal the

length from the point of the shoulder to the furthest extremity of the quarter.

Q. What is the advantage of having a broad forehead ?

A. It generally denotes sense and cleverness.

Q. Why are long nostrils to be desired ?

A. When they are distended in galloping the orifices of the nostrils become wide in proportion to their length when at rest ; and therefore breathing is facilitated.

A horse with a Roman nose is invariably a determined horse, and usually a bold fencer.

Q. What do large ears signify ?

A. A generous, and often a placid temper, especially if they have a tendency to lop. Such horses are always honest, and can be depended upon. A small prick ear is to be regarded with suspicion ; it always means temper, which may be stubbornness or irritability. The one leads to jibbing and such-like vices ; and the other to hot-headedness. If otherwise docile the horse will very likely be a determined puller.

Q. Why should a horse be wide between the angle of the jaws ?

A. Both to give plenty of room for the windpipe, and also to allow freedom to bend the neck to the bit. Good staying racehorses are invariably wide in this respect ; while speedy but short distance ones will often be found rather narrow.

Q. How should the neck be shaped ?

A. It should appear well-balanced, and so put on as to bend well to the bit. Looking at it sideways it should be slightly curved at the throat, but without any appearance of weakness, and be of good length. A short-necked horse, with his head put on like a pickaxe, is ugly to look at and never bridles well. Though the neck should look symmetrical when seen sideways, when seated in the saddle it should appear swelling with muscle, especially just behind the ears. No horse ever stayed yet with a thin, weak neck. There is one conformation that should especially be guarded against, that is "the roarer's neck." A horse that has otherwise a strong neck, but when held tight by the bridle curves it the wrong way at the throat, something like a cob swan does when he proudly sets his sails before his mate, is certain to go a roarer sooner or later, especially if the throat appears particularly thick, almost swollen in fact. There is no possible escape from the malady for such a horse. This formation seems not uncommon in underbred weight-carriers, and hence probably arises the idea that big horses often go roarers ; and also that turning horses out to grass in the summer-time makes them go wrong in their wind. Horses with properly shaped necks will never go roarers through being allowed access to grass—their natural food—and fresh air. The other sort will become roarers under any treatment. The reason appears to be that the nerve connected with the larynx has undue strain put upon it through the unnatural curve of the throat, and as it cannot stretch it gradually loses its vitality, and eventually becomes paralysed.

My attention was directed to this very early in life, as one of the carriage horses had just such a neck, and was a rank roarer. It was impressed upon me then by the old coachman that such necks always ended in roaring, and constant observation since has shown he was right. An amusing occurrence happened when buying remounts during the Boer War from one of the large Southern dealers. Somehow I referred to a roarer's neck, and to my surprise found both the dealer himself and the veterinary surgeon with me had neither of them heard of such a thing. As they appeared incredulous, I said that if a horse should come before me with such a neck I would point it out. Before long such a horse did come up to be looked at, and I at once called attention to it, saying sooner or later it would become a roarer. The horses had all been tried for their wind by the dealer's staff before being shown to us, but of course we satisfied ourselves they were all right before sending them on to the depôt. I shall never forget the look of astonishment that spread over the faces of my two companions when the moment this horse was started to gallop he gave the clearest indications of being wrong in his wind! " I hope to goodness," quoth the dealer, " the Colonel won't pick out any more roarer's necks, for this horse went quite sound when we tried him a day or two ago ! "

Some persons seem to admire this sort of neck, and a deceased friend used to be especially attracted by them, and used to give very long prices for good young hunters so framed ; but I never knew any man possess more horses wrong in their wind, his stable seemed to be quite full of them, and yet he never learned by experience, but continued to buy such horses to the end of his days.

Before leaving the study of necks let me enter a protest against the prevalent custom of hogging the manes of hunters. Although such a practice may be deplored as against all the canons of art, which demand graceful, flowing lines, and not trim, straight ones beloved of dwellers in suburban villas, every one is entitled to follow the dictates of his own taste, and alter the scheme of Nature in any fashion that gives him pleasure. In this case it is so contrary to the owner's own interest to disobey Nature's laws that possibly when this fact is grasped the poor horses may cease to be subjected to a fashion which causes them great discomfort, and even danger. A mane is provided by Nature as a thatch to the vertebræ of the neck, off which the rain will run ; and which will serve as a shade from the summer's sun, and thus prevent sunstroke. To obviate the latter, after first carefully removing what Nature had provided, some thoughtful owners proceed next to purchase sun-bonnets for their horses, which are not nearly so effective as the mane they have done away with, and bear a ludicrous resemblance to a Red Indian in his war-paint and feathers. The greatest inconvenience, however, is caused by the rain, which, instead of running off as it should do, is enabled to penetrate to the very roots of the hair, and cause a serious chill, besides discomfort. No animals can be expected to thrive properly under such conditions. The mountain galloways are accustomed to run out on the fells throughout the roughest storms, but they have thick, shaggy manes, which are like great coats to them, and if deprived of these they would succumb immediately. As a personal matter also, few riders are so secure in their seats they are not glad sometimes to have a mane to clutch hold of, when a bad scramble occurs, and thus save an untimely fall,—but what can they do when the mane is hogged!

Q. It is a common saying that a horse should have length. Can this be obtained without a long back?

A. Most certainly it can. A long back is a disadvantage, as it is necessarily less able to carry weight than a short one, nor is there the same activity with it. A long carriage takes more turning than a shorter one! A horse should have the length beneath, standing over a lot of ground, but there should be only just room on his back to adjust the saddle.

Q. How is this?

A. If his shoulders are well sloped, with the withers running right into the centre of the back, and with long quarters coming well forward, there will be scant room for the saddle. Such a back hardly requires girths, for the saddle will stay in its place of its own accord, and the heart ribs are sure to be deep.

Q. Do these latter make much difference in the position of the saddle?

A. Very much so, for if they are small the saddle is sure to work forward, there being no proper place for the girths. This often happens with young horses, before the frame has properly developed, especially if they have large, round ribs; but as the withers get up, and the heart ribs develop below, the saddle attains its right place.

Q. Is this the reason the girths get so forward with a four-year-old they make sore places behind the elbows?

A. Yes. The best remedy for this state of things is to tie something soft so tightly round the girth that the front edge is kept bent backwards; there is then no longer any friction against the elbow. Nothing is better for this purpose than an old silk bootlace.

Q. Are high withers desirable ?

A. Not unduly high ones, for then they become a source of weakness. Superficial observers are apt to think high withers must mean good shoulders, but this is not necessarily the case.

Q. Please describe what is wanted in the fore-legs.

A. The arms should be long and muscular, and broad just above the knee when seen sideways—a token of strength. The knees should be large, bony, and flat, which implies that the six carpal bones that compose the front of the knee, and the seventh one behind, are well developed, for they have important functions to perform. They not only diminish the shock between the bone of the forearm, and that of the leg, but they fill up the gap between the two when the knee is bent; they are also the points of attachment for certain ligaments and muscles.

Q. Is great bone a necessity in the fore-legs ?

A. The quality of a leg is of much more importance than the mere tape measurement, for soft spongy bone, and gummy sinews, may measure well, and yet give an infinity of trouble to keep right. Moreover, often when persons talk of bone they really mean the whole leg, comprising the sinews as well. It is much more advantageous to have well-developed sinews than extra large bone, for the sinews are the ropes that move the rest. A clean, wiry leg, with the sinews standing out like cords and feeling like wire, is the leg to be desired ; and if it is of a fair size it is better to leave the tape in your pocket ! The bone of the carthorse, and its near descendants, is much more porous than that of the thoroughbred, which resembles ivory in its density. Hence the smaller bone of a well-bred horse may be in reality far stronger than the larger leg of an underbred one.

Q. Do not splints cripple a horse if close to the knee, or touching the sinews ?

A. Splints are most painful things while they are forming, wherever they may be, and it is impossible to know when they have finished the process ! It may take only a few weeks, and it may take two years ! But when they are once really full grown they do not seem to signify in any position, for Nature generally accommodates herself to most things. Though they usually appear on young horses, the writer has more than once had horses throw them out, for the first time, after the age of fourteen ! And though they generally appear on the fore-legs, they will sometimes form on the hind ones. Very often when a horse has developed them when young they will begin to disappear when the animal is nine or ten years old, and finally go away altogether. There are many remedies advertised for their treatment, but though the growth may be delayed, it is very apt to re-commence at a subsequent period.

Sometimes an obscure case of lameness occurs, and it is suspected that the trouble is being caused by the growth of a splint, either an old one that has begun to be active again ; or one just commencing to form, which is frequently the most painful stage, from the stretching of the periosteum. In order to localise the mischief the following ingenious plan is often employed with success : Place the lame leg under a hose of cold water, and keep it there for two or three minutes, until the limb is thoroughly cold ; on removing the hose the seat of inflammation will speedily react and betray itself by its heat, before the remainder of the leg has recovered its normal warmth.

An old Irish remedy is a very simple one, and at any rate does no harm. In the case of a big knee from hitting a stone wall or other mishap, it usually answers well. It is to take a piece of thin sheet-lead, such as comes out of chests of tea, and after smoothing it with the back of a knife to damp the hair of the knee, lay the lead over the place, then put a bandage round it, and finally buckle on a kneecap to keep all in its place. Placed similarly over a splint, and kept there for days, or even weeks, it will sometimes check any further development, making a sweating bandage. But after trying innumerable remedies the writer has come to the conclusion, and has long acted upon it, that the best way is to forget the existence of the animal, and leave it to itself until Nature has settled the matter ; keeping the animal in the meantime in as cheap a manner as is feasible until it is again fit for work. If treatment is desired, two ounces sal-ammoniac may be mixed with half a cup of vinegar and added to a quart of boiling water. This should be put into a bottle when cool, and applied two or three times a day with a sponge, after which a wet bandage must be put on. The intense cold produced will often check the further formation of the splint. Iodine lotion and Rhus Toxico- dendron lotion may also induce the absorbents to remove the bone already formed.

After a day's hunting it is very necessary to search the legs carefully for thorns, especially the knees, and the surest way to detect them is to well wet the hair, and then run the finger up against the way it lies. The smallest thorn can then be felt, if not absolutely imbedded overhead in the skin. It is safer when found to use a pair of pincers to extract it than to endeavour to work it out with the nail, for fear of breaking it. As soon as it has been got out the point should be carefully examined to see if it has been broken off, and if this should be the case a poultice must be applied.

Poultices should not be made, if possible, of bread, or even bran, for when they get dry they get hard, and irritate a wound. Linseed meal, boiled turnips, or carrots mashed up, all make good poultices. The old-fashioned cold-water dressing is as useful as anything for extracting thorns, just a wet linen bandage with oilskin outside ; and this can be applied to parts where the weight of a poultice makes it difficult to keep one in its place. A cabbage leaf makes an ex- cellent substitute for oilskin, and is almost always at hand.

Q. What should be done in the case of a strain of the sinews, or breakdown ?

A. If, as is unfortunately seldom the case, it is possible to attend to the sprain immediately it occurs, before swelling has begun, some application to produce great cold will probably prevent such swelling. taking place, and thereby time is gained ; for afterwards when the inflammation has subsided it is usually necessary to blister the place, to induce the absorbents to remove the deposit which is sure to be left, from the interference with the circulation caused by the swelling. The sal-ammoniac preparation given above is as good as anything for this purpose.

Usually the leg is considerably swollen before the stable is reached, and then there is nothing better than to foment the leg with hot water for a considerable time, to relax the vessels, and allow the circulation to continue its course. The sponge should be pressed against the leg well above the injured part, and the hot water allowed to run down over it. Very hot water is not needed, it being quite sufficient if it feels hot to the hand, but the temperature must be kept up, and not allowed to cool. Any one, though not used to horses, can be impressed to do this, but if assistance cannot be obtained a bucket of hot water, with a rug over it to keep it hot, can usually be elevated sufficiently high for a syphon to be made out of any indiarubber tubing, with the lower end inserted inside a bandage loosely wrapped round the leg. Only a small portion of water should be allowed to flow out at a time, or the bucket will be quickly emptied, and if there is no tap to the end of the tubing, the lower end must be sufficiently choked to regulate the flow. A few straws tied lengthwise round a small stick the thickness of a lead pencil, and thrust inside the tubing, will do as well as anything, and they are always obtainable. Care must be taken that the lower end of the piping is well below the level of the bucket, or the water will not run.

After fomentation a woollen bandage should be soaked in hot water, and put on, and when in its place a few drops of arnica lotion should be poured inside, to run down to the injury. A dry bandage should then be tied round the outside. The fomentation may be repeated the next morning, and then wet bandages dipped in arnica lotion used till all the inflammation has subsided. After the leg has become quite cool a blister will be required, and an excellent one for the purpose is the following :—

No. 1.

Cantharides Pulv.	...	...	1½ drachms.
Adeps ...	...	...	1½ oz.
Ol. Tereb.	...	...	½ drachm.

No. 2.

Hyd. Iodid. Rub.	...	...	1½ drachms.
Adeps ...	...	...	1½ oz.

The two ointments to be made separately, the first (No. 1) being made in a water bath.

The Ol. Tereb. to be put in when cooling.

When made the two are to be mixed together on a slab.

The above blister is the most effectual one the writer has known. When the effects have entirely worn away, and all traces peeled off, which will probably be in about six weeks' time, the blister may be repeated if necessary ; and possibly a third application may be required. Under this treatment, and a long rest, a year if necessary in a very bad case, the leg should get quite right again, without the disfiguring use of the firing iron. At the present moment the writer is using a horse that broke down badly in training, and now it is impossible to distinguish between the two legs in either appearance or by touch, and he has stood work again for a long time. Had the horse been fired he would have been for ever marked out as a screw, and beyond that he would have much deteriorated, for the moment the firing-iron has been laid on the leg, that horse as a racehorse is fully a stone, to two stone, below his former form. This is caused by the contraction of the skin, which never recovers its pristine elasticity after firing, though it does so after blistering. When it is considered that if a horse's stride is only contracted by a couple of inches very many yards will be lost in the course of a mile, it is evident that every other means should be tried to escape this misfortune. The real benefit that results from firing is the enforced rest that is obliged to be given, before it is possible to put the horse into work again. It is the rest, and not the firing, that really completes the cure.

When a horse is blistered it is needful to muzzle it for a few days, or take other pre-cautions, to prevent it gnawing its leg, being provoked to do so by the irritation ; but as soon as this has passed off, and a scab formed, the horse can go out to grass, if such a convenience is at hand, until the leg is ready to be blistered again. It is as well to put a bandage on the leg at first to prevent any mishap.

One reason why firing is often recommended by the groom is that his class believe in heroic measures ; and the owner feels also that at least he has tried the severest remedy he could. The veterinary surgeon gets a good fee for the operation, and is therefore quite willing to fall in with the other's views and substitute firing for blistering, as the animal does not belong to him, and he knows that as much success will probably follow this treatment as any other.

Though the leg may not get perfectly fine, even after three blisterings it should eventually do so, and any thickening that remains may be assisted to depart by applying iodine. The compound liniment should be rubbed in with a brush for about half a minute, for three or four days, until the scarf skin begins to rise. In about four days more the scarf skin ought to fall off, and then the application may be renewed. This is an excellent method of reducing any enlargement after an injury.

It is a very common mistake to imagine a horse has strained the back sinew when he has only struck the back of the foreleg with his hindfoot, either in landing over a fence; or by suddenly striding into very soft boggy ground without being prepared for it. If the blow is a severe one, the appearance is exactly that of a breakdown; the horse will be extremely lame at first, but will be better in a few days, and be as sound as ever. Hence, no doubt, originate some of the marvellous testimonials one sees attached to this or that patent application, for the wonderful cures they have performed within the space of a few hours; but if tested on a real case of breakdown they cannot repeat the success attributed to them, without also the grand remedy of Rest. In the absence of this the whole pharmacopœia remains quite useless.

An infallible test as to whether the swelling has been a blow or a sprain can be decided in a few days, for if the former has been the cause the swelling will mostly have subsided except over the immediate place that has been struck, and here a lump will remain, at first almost the size of a walnut in a severe case, and afterwards reduced to the dimensions of a hazel-nut. For months afterwards this can be felt, and at the next growth of the coat probably a few white hairs will appear at that spot; if it has been a breakdown the thickening, on the contrary, will extend to the whole length of the sinew.

Often after a blow the mud on the leg will, on examination, show an altered appearance where the foot has struck, and thereby indicate what has taken place.

Q. Of what use are the splint bones ?

A. Of none now ; but the primeval horse is stated to have had eight legs, and the splint bones no doubt then supported the extra limbs. It is possible the supplementary legs were of assistance in traversing boggy ground and morasses, which are believed to have been more plentiful at that remote period than now, in the same way the extra toes at the back of a cow's fetlock help her in soft places at the present time. An interesting example of reversion to the primitive type was that of a mare which was racing in 1822–23, and ran in nine races, two of which she won. She was first named Pincushion, which was afterwards changed to Creeping Jenny. She suddenly commenced to throw out a new set of limbs which commenced half way below the hocks, on the hind legs ; and from just above the fetlock on the near foreleg.

But as one swallow does not make a summer,

and on the principle that a motion always requires to be seconded, another example can be given to show that such weird creatures are still to the fore. Dr. Wilson, of Kirkby Overblow, in Yorkshire, has been kind enough to write me this letter, concerning a horse he lately had in his possession :—

"*March* 26, 1905.

" DEAR SIR,—In answer to your inquiry about the horse with five feet, I had one (but sold him about nine years ago) which had a large scar on one fore fetlock, extending down into the hoof in the form of a large fissure, which was said to be where a fifth foot had been growing when foaled. This horse my predecessor here had bought from T. Secker, the vet. at Borobridge, so I suppose this account would be true. The scar was on the inner aspect of the off foreleg, and the foot was slightly contracted. The pastern was rather upright, and the fetlock joint a little stiff, so that if he galloped putting that foot to the ground first, he shook you a little. He was a very good hunter, and a sound, hard horse.

" I lost sight of him about four years ago, and suppose he must be now dead, as he was an old horse when I knew him."

I feel quite thankful that, when I followed the occupation of a trainer, no owner had the temerity to send a horse with nearly as many legs as a centipede to be trained ! Those with only the normal number of four legs caused quite enough anxiety, but if a few of them had resembled Creeping Jenny the strain would have been too much for any peaceful man !

Q. Is there anything special to be noted about the fetlocks?

A. It is not wise to clip away the long hair from the back of the fetlocks, which is intended by Nature to drain away water from the heels, and if left alone is a great preventative of cracked heels. People do not seem in many cases to believe that it is better to leave Nature's arrangements alone, for she has invariably thought the thing well out, while the person who makes a drastic change to gratify a whim has usually never given a single thought to the subject at all, and is often not really a practical man.

The fetlocks are a most likely place to be struck by the opposite foot if the conformation is not quite perfect. They should then be protected by some form of boot ; but attention should also be directed to so altering the tread of the affected leg that the fetlock is slightly inclined away from the offending hoof. This can be only done by thickening the inside quarter of the shoe, so as to throw the weight of the body more on the outside of the foot. Persons who do not reflect deeply are apt to alter the shoe of the offending foot, but beyond taking care that it does not project in the least beyond the crust, and is instead kept well within it, nothing can be done, except lightening the shoe altogether, in hopes that the action may be raised a little higher and so miss the place. Almost a hair's breadth will sometimes make all the difference. Many a horse that hits himself badly with ordinary shoes will escape scot free when shod on the Charlier system.

A very practical way of detecting what part of the shoe is doing the mischief is to mix some flour and water to the consistency of thick cream, and dab it on the fetlock. On trotting the horse and twisting him round, some of the white paste is sure to adhere to the opposite foot at the spot sought for.

There are two forms of boots that answer well as a protection against brushing. One is often called a " Yorkshire boot," and is made out of a piece of old horse rug. To be effective it requires some care in cutting out. It should be long enough to overlap when placed round the fetlock, and the four corners should at first project a little beyond the middle, when laid flat. It may be fastened either with tape or a small strap (which is the better plan), but whichever method is chosen, the material should be sewn, for two or three inches in the middle, to the rug, and rather nearer the upper edge than half-way. Close to the edges of the narrow sides of the rug loops of tape should be placed, through which the ligature will pass, and thus keep the boot from drooping when in use. To adjust the boot it must be placed fully upright round the fetlock, with the ligature on the outside, which is then fastened loose enough for the forefinger to be passed under the boot ; the upper part is then reversed over the ligature and neatly arranged. Should it now appear there is more material than necessary, a little judicious trimming with a pair of scissors will soon put things right. The only objection to this boot is that in deep arable some mud will occasionally work into lumps inside, under the ligature, and the friction that ensues may make a tender place.

This objection does not apply to the other boot mentioned, which is simply two pieces of leather, shaped to the fetlock, which only cover the inside and outside of the joint, leaving the front and rear part bare. Each piece of leather is cut in a semicircular form at the lower edge; the upper part being attached to a strap, that buckles round the fetlock. This is a most excellent boot, and when it gets hit, and revolves, the other side comes into the vacant place; while no dirt can lodge behind it.

Q. The pasterns are the next consideration. What should be their formation?

A. They should be strong, and nicely sloped, the horse standing well up on them. Straight pasterns are uncomfortable to ride upon, as a horse soon goes proppy upon them; and they do not suit deep ground. Long pasterns, on the contrary, are deliciously easy for the rider, but are only suitable for riding on firm grass land; in deep ground a horse with such pasterns is almost helpless, and very likely to over-reach.

On the way the pasterns combine with the fetlocks depends whether the action is true or not. If they are out of the direct line, the toe will either turn in—pigeon-toed—or turn out; and it is in this latter case that brushing is most likely to occur. With the former malformation a horse is usually slow; but often with the latter great speed is associated. Pasterns are often the seat of ringbone, which is the same bony growth on them that is termed a splint when it occurs on the leg (or cannon) bone. The pastern is composed of two separate bones which fit into each other, and the upper bone is always rather prominent at the point of articulation. Sometimes this is rather extra developed, and then is frequently mistaken for a case of ringbone. The position of the enlargement, and the fact that both the pasterns are alike in this respect (are a pair, in fact), should be a guide to prevent this error of judgment being made.

Sometimes an obscure case of lameness is caused by a deposit taking place at the back of the pastern ; in a difficult case a careful examination should invariably be made of this part, which often is overlooked.

Cracked heels sometimes extend to the back of the fetlock. They are caused partly by the leg not being dried after being wet through washing or otherwise, and partly by the horse being gross. A horse subject to them should never have his heels wetted if it can be helped. Zinc ointment may be applied to them to allay the irritation, and a dose of

Epsom salts	...	...	...	2 oz.
Common salt	...	...	...	½ oz.

given twice a week in a mash, until improvement is effected. Before going out to work a horse should have plenty of vaseline rubbed into the cracked heel to soften the skin, or the cracks will be made worse.

Q. We have now arrived at the feet. Surely they must be difficult to keep in good order ?

A. This is quite true, and neglect can soon cause the soundest feet to go wrong. When it is considered what an inelastic box of horn the outer covering consists of, it is obvious that if any swelling takes place inside from inflammation, congestion, or suppuration, the pain inseparable from these conditions must be greatly increased, and also the difficulty of affording relief.

The feet must always be very carefully washed out whenever the horse returns to the stable, no dirt of any sort being allowed to lodge anywhere, and this is where a careless groom so often fails. The mud that has been picked up is too often not entirely removed from about the frog, and then gets saturated with ammonia from the wet straw in the stable, and the frog soon begins to get diseased. There was much to be said in favour of the old fashion of stopping horses' feet, which acted as a preventive of their getting them filled with their own droppings, which are very prejudicial, especially to the hind feet; if any stopping is used it had better be of tow, steeped in a little tar, but a better plan, if the feet are healthy, is merely to grease them after washing. Once or twice a week all the feet should be dressed over with an ointment composed of honey, tar, and elder ointment, mixed in equal proportions, which will be found to keep the feet in excellent order, if regularly attended to.

The objection to stopping feet, and also to bedding them on sawdust, or peat mould when it has crumbled up into dust, is that they all prevent air freely reaching the sole of the hoof, and when this is the case the horn is apt to become rather spongy and soft. When in this state the horse is apt to flinch when treading on sharp stones on a hard road. Bedding should always be of some porous material as straw, fresh fibrous peat, or wood shavings. These last make an excellent bedding, though their appearance is against them; but it has the advantage that

horses do not eat it. When peat moss is used
it is a good plan to place a thin layer of straw on
the top, for the horse to stand upon. Sea sand is
very objectionable, for horses are tempted to
swallow it, for the sake of the salt contained
in it. When any material is used that will
cake in the hoof, the middle of the bed should
be laid bare each day, and thrown up against
the sides for several hours while the horse stands
on the bare floor, which will prevent the horn
getting into a soft condition.

The horn of the hoof begins growing at the
coronet (where the hair of the fetlock ceases)
and proceeds downwards in long fibres, which
form a very thin wall at first but thicker below,
until they reach the ground, where they form
a thin rim all round the hoof, and it is within
this thin wall the smith must drive his nails,
for the interior space is filled up with the
lamella, and the coffin bone (the bone of the
foot). If the nails go inward too far, lameness is
the result. The nails should never be allowed to
be driven high up, for the danger of pricking
the horse is so much increased ; but often a horse
gets pricked without any nail hole to show it, for
as soon as the horse has flinched the smith has
withdrawn the nail before it has come through
to the outside. If a horse goes lame, or tender,
after it has been shod the nails should at once
be drawn, and the shoe taken off, and a poultice
put on for a few hours. If the nails are carefully
examined as each one is drawn, the offending one
may be frequently detected at first, by being
slightly discoloured towards the upper end, and
looking moist. It may be that the nail has not
actually traversed through the sensitive part, but

is impinging upon it sufficiently to make the horse go tender.

The rim round the sole, composed of the long fibres of the horn, would naturally be worn gradually away through the friction with the ground, if it was not protected by the shoe; and it was from this that Mr. Charlier founded his system of shoeing. It is the best system in practice that has ever been devised, only it requires such care in doing it cannot be trusted to an ordinary smith.

A "sandcrack" consists of a splitting of the fibres from the bottom of the hoof upwards. The remedy for this is a horizontal incision above the apex of the sandcrack, to prevent the lesion extending higher up the hoof; and also using a bar shoe, instead of the ordinary one, to prevent as far as possible any extension of the hoof, for in spite of its unyielding appearance the horny box does contract and expand to a slight degree, each time the weight comes upon it in progression. A mild blister round the coronet should also be applied, to stimulate the production of stronger fibres, and then nothing more can be done without veterinary assistance, if the above means fail; and patience must be exercised until the crack gradually disappears on reaching the bottom of the hoof. It takes from ten months to a year for the whole hoof to be reproduced from the coronary band.

Another disease of the fibrous horn is that of "seedy toe." A hollow is formed underneath the superficial covering, which is not visible to the eye, and the horn is gradually eaten away by some of the invisible organisations of which we hear so much nowadays. If not checked, the mischief will spread, and the horse be temporarily incapacitated for work. The blacksmith's knife must be evoked, and every particle of diseased horn cut out, and then a few drops of turpentine, or butyr of antimony poured over the surface, though this last must be used with care and discretion. The cavity must be kept constantly dressed with tar ointment, and in the course of time it will grow out similar to a sandcrack. The horn composing the sole of the foot is quite different in texture from the rest, and instead of wearing away by attrition, it flakes off in large particles. There is no need for the smith to touch this with his knife at all ; he does no good ; but if he contents himself with just removing what would otherwise come off by itself, he does no harm. He is very apt, however, to make "a clean job of it," and pare the foot well out. Beneath the sole the horn gradually becomes a soft, cheese-like substance, which is all that covers the sensitive part, so that by the time the smith has finished, there is sometimes not much left to interpose between the shock of half a ton or more (the weight of the horse), and the jagged edges of a newly-macadamised road.

In my childhood it was the fashion for a smith to pare out the foot till the sole would spring to his thumb, and many a time have I stood and watched the man pressing with his thumb, and then paring off a little more sole, until he thought there was sufficient " spring." If he had had his own boots taken off, and it was found that his feet when pressed sprung well through his stockings, and he had been started in them to run over a new metalled road, he might perhaps have gained a clearer idea about the result of his treatment of a horse !

The frog requires great care, for it is the cushion of the foot to prevent jar. It should have the ragged portions just neatly trimmed off, lest they become pockets to contain dirt, when suppuration is often set up ; but nothing more should be cut away than is absolutely necessary. Neglect will encourage suppuration in the cleft (which is termed " thrush ") ; but if the frog is constantly dressed with the tar ointment there should be no danger of its occurrence. When, however, it is found to be present, and there is an offensive discharge, sulphate of copper should be applied in the proportion of half an ounce of sulphate of copper to six ounces of tar.

If the frog is very extensively diseased, all the affected part should be cut away until sound horn is reached, even to the extent, if necessary, of paring down to the quick. A new sound frog will soon grow. In this case a bar shoe must be put on for a few weeks, until the new frog is sufficiently grown to perform its proper functions. The tar dressing should be continually used, as long as necessary.

Over the frog, in the interior of the foot, and behind the junction of the lower pastern and coffin bone, is situated the little navicular bone whose chief function is to lessen the jar of concussion to the leg. It not unfrequently becomes the seat of disease in itself, for which nothing much can be done ; though any foot lameness is often called navicular through ignorance. A horse suffering from this complaint usually rests his foot on the toe, taking all the weight he can off the heel. When exercised he goes chiefly on his toes, and though hardly able to move at first, the lameness generally wears off in soft ground as he gets warm, but is worse the next day. If of long standing, look for small circular ridges on the inside only of the foot, which indicate inflammation at different stages. A horse that has been out at grass may also have circular ridges, which arise from an unequal growth of the horn according as the weather has been wet or dry; but these ridges will go all round the foot. Lastly, the affected foot when at rest will generally be intensely cold, while all the other three feet will be of one temperature and comparatively warm.

In "laminitis," on the contrary, or "fever in the feet," the affected foot will be far hotter than the others; while the horse will be almost glued to the ground if the attack is acute. It is a case for the advice of a veterinary surgeon, but if beyond the reach of one the treatment formerly recommended by Mr. Broad, veterinary surgeon of Bath, though it appears cruel at first sight, is justified by success. It consists of forcing the horse to walk for half an hour, and when the increased circulation has lessened the congestion and consequent pain so that he can move almost freely, he must be taken back to the stable, and his feet placed in a cold bath for an hour to prevent swelling and consequent congestion taking place again. At the end of the hour in the bath the horse must take a second walk for an hour, and then again stand in the bath. This treatment must be continued daily until no longer necessary, on the improvement of the animal.

The heels are liable to "over-reach," that is a blow of the hind foot causes a bruise. If it is a severe one a poultice should be put on, after the wound has been washed clean, and any torn bits of hair or horn cut away. The next day a little iodoform may be dusted over the place, or other antiseptic applied, if there is an open wound ; but if it is merely a bruise, nothing better can be applied than the old nursery ointment " pomade divine."

Corns are a bruise upon the sole of the foot, at the angle between the wall and the bar. They are usually caused from the shoe being nailed on too tight, so that as the horn grows the shoe becomes imbedded in it, and cannot " give " at all, when the weight of the body comes upon the foot. Another cause is dirt or grit getting in between the shoe and the foot. Cutting away the bars, so as to give the appearance of a more broad and open foot, is also a cause. This is a mischievous practice, for the bars are Nature's plan to prevent the heels from contracting, and every care should be taken to preserve them intact.

Pressure with the smith's pincers will speedily disclose the presence of corns, for the horse will flinch at once if they exist. They should be at once cut out, and the cavity filled with a little tow and tar ointment. If matter has formed a free vent must be made, and a poultice applied, or a quittor may form and under-run the sole, or make its appearance at the coronet.

Q. If the heels should begin to contract, how can this be prevented ?

A. By either shoeing the horse with three-quarter tips ; or what is still better by putting on short Charlier shoes. The object is to bring pressure upon the frog and heels.

Q. Should not the elbow be well clear of the ribs ?

A. Yes, it is a serious fault if the animal is tied in at the elbows. Another thing that also should be noticed is when the leg is bent back from the knee, the foot should almost clear the elbow outside. When this is the case, and the elbow is well clear of the ribs, the action will be quite free.

Q. Do not the withers sometimes get galled on the top ?

A. This is caused either by the saddle being too wide in the tree, and consequently pressing upon the withers; or by having ill-fitting clothing, the breast-girth being too tight over the points of the shoulders, and the roller so tightly buckled that the rug is always taut over the withers, and this is the more common cause of the two. There should always be room enough to pass a finger freely under the pommel when the rider is in the saddle, and more room is desirable. An injury here is hard to heal, there being nothing but fibrous tissue over the bones. If the saddle seems to be too low down, a saddle cloth, or numnah, must be placed underneath, or some substitute for one.

A capital treatment for wrung withers, or a galled back, is to mix two teaspoonfuls of salt in a teacupful of vinegar, and apply as soon as the saddle is taken off. Afterwards continue to use the vinegar daily, without the salt, sponging the injury freely, and finally placing a cabbage leaf over it, to prevent evaporation.

If there is a sore place, the skin being broken, a little iodoform should be dusted over it, or finely powdered alum, and fullers earth, through a piece of fine muslin.

Iodoform is a great boon in all cases of wounds, such as broken knees, or injuries from stakes, as it is so easily applied, and is an excellent antiseptic. A convenient way to apply it is with a small, common garden tobacco puff, such as is used for destroying green-fly. Iodoform being a light powder, requires a heavier one united with it to make the puff act properly, and borax powder answers well for this purpose ; enough should be added to make the powder blow out freely, instead of caking inside. Deep wounds are apt to close too quickly, and must be probed daily to keep them open, for which an ordinary tallow candle often answers. A "halfpenny dip" is sufficiently firm to force its way in, while there is nothing hard about it to do any injury. After it has been inserted, warm water with some soft soap dissolved in it (which is a useful disinfectant) should be squirted in to cleanse the interior, and then some iodoform puffed inside; or some antiseptic lotion used instead.

Q. If a wound has healed up from the bottom, but still does not form a scab and heal properly, what should be done ?

A. Sometimes there is too much granulation, and purple pimples ("proud flesh") appear, and require drying up before it will heal. A little powdered sulphate of copper (bluestone) dusted two or three times over the place will eradicate the proud flesh, and cause the wound to heal. This condition usually arises from there having been too much fomentation, or too prolonged poulticing. Sometimes the wound looks greasy but still does not heal, and this may be treated with a little powdered alum and fullers earth, dusted over as described above.

Q. How should broken knees be treated ?

A. The knee should be well washed with warm water to remove all the dirt, and then poulticed for a day or two, till the wound has a clean raw surface. Each time the poultices are changed a little warm water and soft soap should be gently squirted over the wound, from a glass syringe.

As soon as the inflammation has subsided the poultices must be stopped, and iodoform puffed over the surface after it has daily been cleaned by syringing. A piece of linen with the surface well covered with cold cream, or zinc ointment, to prevent it sticking to the wound, may be fastened lightly above and below the knee, to keep dirt out ; but no flies will come near to irritate the horse when iodoform is used. A cradle should be put round the horse's neck, to prevent it gnawing the wound.

Q. Should not a horse be well ribbed up ?

A. Certainly, but the last rib must not approach too close to the prominent part of the hip (the ilium), or the horse cannot bring his hind leg properly under him, either in galloping or jumping. There should be sufficient space in the hollow between the two to contain the doubled-up fist, with the thumb extended as far as possible. With many cobby animals there is not enough space for the fist alone. The back ribs themselves can be just as large in the one case, as in the other. Even of more importance, as far as constitution is concerned, than the length

of the ribs, is the way they spring from the
spine, and a horse whose ribs arch well out is
often a hardier animal than a more slab-sided
one, though the latter may have the larger ribs.
What is wanted is what is often called " a good
spur place," in the homely language of the stable.
Light back ribs are almost always the sign of a
delicate animal, and this is invariably true of
a gelding, though not always so of mares if they
are deep in their heart ribs ; and these latter
frequently stay well in racing.

Q. Is a roach back a favourable sign for
jumping ?
A. Usually it is, and it is the only redeeming
point in a long-backed animal. But there is
nothing better than a good flat broad back, resembling a ram's.

Q. Should the croup be level with the back ?
A. Not for galloping or hunting. It is a
distinguishing mark of a Yorkshire coach-horse.
All fast racehorses droop somewhat in the croup,
and so do Arabians invariably. This is not
necessary for an elevated carriage of the tail,
which gives such an air of fashion and symmetry
to a horse, though it certainly simulates extra
length. It is to make a miserable imitation of
this that induces people to cut most of their
horses' tails off, in order that they may elevate
the stumps. To the skilled eye the effect is a
caricature, and ludicrous !

Q. What other objections are there to the
practice of docking ?
A. That when a horse is turned out to grass,
either to summer it, or after an illness, or as a
brood mare, the poor animal has been deprived

of its only weapon against the attack of flies ; and the constant stamping in consequence that is required to get rid of them, is prejudicial to the legs, and does away with much of the good that would otherwise be obtained from the run at grass.

Nature devised the tail partly to harmonise with the neck and head of the horse, in the general outline, and make up a symmetrical whole ; for if the frame of the body, with the four legs as posts to support it, is carefully looked at, then a prolongation at one end demands another at the other end, to make the figure balance. Logically, therefore, if one end is shortened, so ought the other to be in equal proportion ; and if the tail is cut off, then the head and neck should be cut off too ! Otherwise the result is much the same as a teapot with a spout intact, but with a broken handle ! No wonder foreigners still look upon us as a barbarous race, as in the days of Voltaire !

> " Vous fiers Anglois,
>   Barbares que vous êtes,
>   Coupez la tête aux rois
>   Et la queue à vos bêtes ;
>   Mais les François,
>   Polis et droits,
>   Aimant les lois,
>   Laissent la queue aux bêtes
>   Et la tete à leurs rois."

Unfortunately for the truth of the satire these lines were penned a little too previous ! but at the time they were written the horrors of the Revolution had not yet taken place, and the brilliant Frenchman was both witty and right. What advance have we made in matters of taste, in the interval that has elapsed ?

There is another aspect of the question of docking horses, whether the loss of the tail does not somewhat detract from an animal's power of turning, for it is common knowledge that the most brilliant greyhound is of no use for coursing if it breaks, or loses part of, its tail. It is not unlikely that to a certain extent the tail acts as a balancing pole to a horse also. One of the little dodges to test the strength of a horse's spine is to stand behind him, and taking hold of the end of the tail to judge by the resistance he can offer to your raising it upright what the strength of his spine is. There is a great difference in the power of different horses in this respect ; and it must be a severe shock to the nervous system when deprived of this part of the structure. How the nervous system is affected, and what a loss there is of power through docking, may be seen any day after a sharp gallop when the stumps of short-docked horses are seen shaking so unpleasantly, it is painful to look at them ; while those horses that belong to humane owners, and have not been deprived of their natural appendages on account of unreasoning fashion, appear calm and happy. Occasionally, no doubt, there are cases when a horse's dock is twisted on one side, or is abnormally long, and then two or three inches may be excised with advantage to the general appearance. The tail will still appear full and long, as if the operation had not been performed ; though when using it to sweep off a fly the horse must feel as much hampered by the loss of the flexible end as a fly-fisherman would do if he

was deprived of the top joint of his rod. The
recognised length of the hair of the tail for
hunters, before this present fashion of docking
set in a few years ago, was to reach to the
bottom of the thighs, when hanging naturally
down. It is then sufficiently short, when raised
in the walk, to be out of the reach of the mud,
while the graceful swing of the tail, as it keeps
time to the stride of a well-bred horse, gives a
charming air of swagger to the animal, and is
very taking. All this is lost by docking the
horse so short that only a stump is left.

Q.   What is to be noted in the quarters ?
A.   They should be very muscular and long,
for on the length of a muscle depends its
retractile power. Standing behind the horse the
thighs should be seen to meet, for a narrow split-
up horse can never do a long, hard day's work.
Especially, too, should the triceps muscle show
great development and roundness, the muscle
that, looking from behind at the outline of the
quarter in the direction of the stifle, gives the
roundness to that part. The thigh should run
into the second thigh, and the latter continue
to the hock, something in the shape of a V ;
that is, the change from one to the other should
be so gradual, it is difficult to tell by the eye
where one ends and the other begins. In many
horses, on the contrary, the thigh ends abruptly,
and the second thigh is the same width all the
way to the hock. This is due to the extra
development, or the reverse, of two important
little muscles at the bottom of the thigh, which
unite, and pass as one tendon to the point of the
hock. This answers to the " tendon Achilles " in

man, for the hock joint, in anatomy, corresponds to the human heel. A great deal depends on that tendon; and its strength depends on the development of the aforesaid muscles.

Q. Now that we have arrived at the hocks, please state how they should be formed.

A. They must be large, wide, and well-developed, with a prominent "point," which is the lever to straighten the leg. An increase in the length of the lever adds considerably to the force of the spring. The diseases they chiefly suffer from are spavin, bog spavin, curbs, and thorough-pins.

Spavins are the same sort of bony formation, on the inside of the hocks, as are splints and ringbones in their respective places. If a spavin does not interfere with the working of a joint, when it is once fully developed the horse may work for a long time without much, if any, detriment; but usually there is more or less stiffness in the joint. There are various ways of detecting its presence. If sufficiently large to be visible, a good method is to stand in front of the horse, stoop down, and look between the forelegs at the hocks, when any deviation from the normal can be seen plainly. Sometimes one of the small bones has an extra development, which, at first sight, appears like a spavin; but the touch should diagnose if this is the case, as well as the fact that both hocks are alike. Such hocks are termed "strong hocks," and are usually very sound ones. The touch, when educated, is a surer guide to the detection of spavin than sight. If a horse is apt to resent his hocks being felt, a foreleg should be held up whilst the examination is being made. The proper manner to do this is to raise the foot almost as high as the elbow, and then hold the tip of the toes, bending the fetlock a little back. The horse is then helpless to resist, and very little effort is needed to retain the foot in position ; but if the horse is allowed to get his leg down on a level with his knee, and is held by the pastern, he can snatch his foot away, even from a very strong grasp.

The most certain way of detecting whether a spavin is likely to be troublesome is to pick up that leg, and holding the hoof in both hands press the leg up against the body for about a minute, keeping the hock well flexed. Then let the leg down, and have the horse immediately trotted, when he will at once show lameness if a spavin is in fault. A " bog spavin " is a soft swelling in front of the hock. It is also called a " jack spavin." Many good hunters have this, and work on for years without suffering inconvenience.

Curbs are a great nuisance, especially with young horses. As they get older they frequently grow out of them ; but a horse with weak hocks, having a piece cut out of the shank, as it were, just below the joint in front, is always liable to spring a curb.

It is a sprain of the ligaments at the back of the hock, about four inches below the point, where a swelling may be felt, with heat and soreness. It happens instantaneously, frequently from a sudden slip in galloping, especially in deep ground ; and very often also with a young horse, from catching his toe when trotting along, especially when tired.

A lotion of salt and vinegar may be applied, as

recommended for a galled back, and when the inflammation has subsided, the blister should be rubbed on that was recommended after a breakdown. When the effects of this have passed off Compound Tincture of Iodine, or a lotion made from Rhus Toxicodendron, should be applied until all signs of the curb have disappeared. Otherwise a permanent swelling will remain, causing disfigurement for life.

An old-fashioned and effective sweating blister for curbs was to apply a cabbage-leaf to the place, immediately the horse was brought back to the stable.

Thorough-pin is the name given to a bursal enlargement at the side of the hock, but beyond the disfigurement it does not interfere with work. The Rhus Toxicodendron lotion has a good effect in reducing this and other bursal enlargements. It should be painted on for three or four days, when the scarf skin will rise as when iodine is used ; and a similar rest must be given, and then the application renewed again, and again, till the swelling is reduced. If a horse is turned out to grass for a few weeks it will usually be found that thorough-pins, capped hocks, elbows, &c., will disappear when the animal comes into the stable again, and is fed on dry food. After being relaxed at grass, there seems to be a general bracing up of the system on returning again to the stable. If a horse is given to capping his hocks when lying down, or capping his elbows, he should wear a hock cap for the first ailment ; and for the second have a padded roll of leather buckled round his fetlock, which will prevent his lying on his shoe, the usual cause of a capped elbow.

Q. How should hunters be treated in the summer-time ?

A. There are three ways of dealing with them; either to turn them into a loose box for some months, keep them in steady work all through the summer, or put them out to grass.

Q. What are the arguments for and against these different methods ?

A. To begin with the first, there are many grave objections to this, and it cannot be recommended. If a horse is kept in a loose box for three or four months without any exercise, every muscle and sinew gets so relaxed, it is impossible to have him really fit before the end of the hunting season. It must be remembered that the heart and lungs are muscular, and they share in the general relaxation. In ordinary hunting it is not possible to define with exactness how much a horse may have degenerated, or come on, but with a racehorse this is comparatively easy with the assistance of trials. A horse kept for four months in a loose box would be fully six months before he would be fit to race with success ; and would much more likely require a whole year before he was at the top of his form again. So much fat accumulates about the heart and kidneys, in such a prolonged state of idleness, that the process of getting rid of this must be very gradually attempted, or serious mischief may ensue. In addition to this the tendons are in a relaxed state, and are in danger of being strained ; and however careful the attendant may be, the horse is certain to jump about and lark, when he first begins work, from joy at being released from his long confinement.

Passing on to the next plan, that of keeping a horse in steady work throughout the summer, there is a great deal to be said in favour of it, horses so treated being fit to take the field almost at once, only requiring a few sharp gallops to make them ready to follow hounds; for their tendons and muscles are ready to stand the strain of hard work without further preparation. One great argument against it, where there are a large number of horses in the stud, is that of expense; for almost as many men are required to look after and exercise the horses, as in the hunting season, while the consumption of hay and straw is about the same.

Where only two or three horses are kept it answers very well, for they can be used for hacks, or light harness work, with much benefit to their ultimate condition; though in these days of bicycles a hack is very seldom required in the summer-time, while motors must more and more each year militate against the use of horses and carriages, for a pleasure-drive. Dwellers in the wilder parts, where rough, hilly ground has often to be traversed, impassable to mechanical vehicles, will soon be almost the only persons who will do any riding except in the hunting season. Old horses, whose joints are beginning to get shaky, are not benefited by work in the summer; and the risk of accidents when at exercise has further to be taken into consideration.

After weighing all things, the system of turning horses out to graze, if carried out under proper conditions, answers the best, for the muscular development is kept up; due circulation of the blood from daily exercise is ensured; and the effect of the change of food from dry stimulating corn and hay to juicy grass, combined with continuous fresh air, acts as a most invigorating restorative to the legs and constitution, that have become jaded through overwork in the hunting-field. Turning out to grass must, however, be done with discretion. Rich, luscious herbage, that would speedily convert a trek-ox into beef, is not the sort most suitable for horses, that are soon to do fast work again. Nor is a tiny paddock a proper place, without any change for the whole summer, though if there are two or three such pastures, where constant change can be given from one to another, they may answer very well. Horses are most benefited by having a considerable range, where they are not continually confronted with the same blades of grass ; and the herbage should be comparatively scanty, so that a horse cannot fill himself full in a short time, but must, on the contrary, work hard for his dinner, and take a long time in obtaining it. There should be a plentiful supply of good water from a pond, or stream, easily accessible. The land preferably should be undulating, and in a bracing locality, for horses, like human beings, are very sensitive to a relaxing climate, or the reverse.

Where there is an extensive range, horses will be observed to be feeding the greater part of each twenty-four hours ; and if undisturbed will wander round in ordered routine, so that at any given hour they will be found feeding at the same identical place, day after day, unless the weather is such that shelter is needed from the elements. The more change there is in the character of the soil, and consequently in the herbage, the more they will appreciate it, and thrive upon it.

When, however, horses are kept in very tiny paddocks of half an acre or so, their food being supplemented with hay, and perhaps a little corn, it will be observed that after grazing a short time they get tired of doing so, and either wander about looking for company, or stand listlessly at the gate, or door, of the field. Such paddocks cannot compete with large pastures in the benefit to be obtained from a summer's run.

Often, when many horses are turned out together, a particular animal will be so troublesome with the others it is better to remove it, with another for a companion, to a separate field ; and sometimes also a set will be made against an individual, whose life is made a burden to it, and it cannot thrive if perpetually bullied. This, and another, should therefore be put somewhere by themselves. Of course, all hind-shoes must be removed before they are turned out, so that an ill-natured kick cannot do any serious mischief. Fore-shoes are, however, generally better left on, especially in any case where the hoofs are brittle, and break away badly at the toes. It will nearly always be found that each horse has a special pal amongst the others, and that these two keep constantly in company when grazing, frequently having their noses almost touching each other, and such predilections should be carefully noted and sedulously fostered.

Before horses are turned out it is necessary that they should be ungroomed for at least four or five days, so that the natural grease may accumulate in the coat, resembling a quantity of dust if the hair is parted a little, which is their natural protection against wet and cold. If a horse was turned out in bad weather without this precaution it would speedily get a chill, when serious consequences might ensue if left out in this state. It is rare for a horse properly prepared to catch cold when at grass, except from an epidemic of strangles, or influenza ; but if a horse is observed with a cold, it should at once be taken into the stable and nursed till recovered.

It is sometimes put forward by persons of limited experience that horses turned out to grass are liable to become roarers in consequence, but such a catastrophe need not be feared when a horse is sound and of good conformation. It has been previously pointed out that the shape of certain throats renders it almost a matter of certainty that some day roaring will supervene under any conditions ; and the necessarily relaxed state of the body consequent on living on grass entirely, must include the throat as well as other organs, and possibly may dispose the malady to make an appearance earlier than it would otherwise have done. But such a horse would scarcely escape his fate under any conditions in this climate, and it would be hardly fair to attribute a case of roaring entirely to having been out at grass, without the whole of the attendant circumstances being known, and duly weighed. Out of thousands of horses turned out to grass in the writer's experience, there has not been one single case of roaring follow in consequence. It may here be mentioned that, amongst many other winners, " Belmont " won for the writer the Dunboyne Plate at Fairyhouse, and the Conyngham Cup at Punchestown, after being turned out to grass the previous summer ; while " Monkshood " won the Grand National Hunters'

Steeplechase, run that time at Derby, after having been kept up, and worked quietly, instead of being turned out. As the two latter are both four-mile steeplechases, the systems under which each horse was summered cannot be far wrong ; nor can there be much choice between them. Both races were very severely contested, so that the horses must have been at their very best to prove successful. Had either of them been summered in a loose box, it is very improbable that it would have been within hail of the winner, when it passed the post.

Gritty, sandy soils are not suitable for horses, especially in a dry summer, when pastures are very shrunk, and horses consequently bite too close to the ground. Sand taken into the stomach causes anæmia, and finally diarrhœa. If there is any doubt about the cause, the sand can easily be detected in the droppings if carefully examined. The horse must be removed from the place, and given bran mashes and linseed oil until recovered.

Except for the danger of taking cold in chilly weather, there is no harm in horses wading into a pond to obtain the water plants of which they are very fond, and on which they seem to thrive ; certainly they are very partial to them, and often prefer them to the sweetest grass.

There is one inconvenience, however, that must always be expected, the swallowing the eggs of internal parasites, and a vermifuge is often needed after a run at grass. The success of this depends almost entirely on the horse being deprived of all food for twenty-four hours, so that the intestines are quite empty, before the administration of the medicine. There is nothing better than the well-tried remedy of turpentine and oil, but it is very necessary that the turpentine is thoroughly incorporated with the oil, being broken up into minute globules before being administered. It is a good plan to mix the turpentine first with the white of a raw egg, putting them both into a soda-water bottle, and giving them careful and energetic shaking before adding them to the linseed oil. Turpentine amalgamates more readily with white of egg than it does with oil. This is especially suited to the long round worms, and the small ones with pointed tails. It is wise to follow the physic with a course of Harvey's aconite powders, which are so well known.

The worst enemy is the bot, for no remedy seems to have any effect upon it; and to its unsuspected presence is due much of the unthriftiness that is often looked upon as a necessary consequence of turning a horse out in the summer; and the recommendation to give him a winter's run instead, though backed up undoubtedly by the light of experience, is really due to not having safeguarded the animal in the summer-time from the attacks of the bot-fly (the Œstrus Equi).

It is surprising to see the indifference with which this pest is regarded, even by those from whom more care would be naturally expected. Often when visiting horses at grass, at the period when the parent fly is actively engaged in laying her eggs, quantities of the latter may be seen adhering to the horses' coats, only waiting to be licked off and transferred to the animal's interior, to undergo the next period of their life stages. In the fields of skilful, educated farmers; in those of owners of large studs, who employ expensive stud-grooms to manage their stables; and in the paddocks of breeders of blood-stock, may be found any day in the season numbers of animals doomed to go through many months of gradual wasting away of flesh and condition, which is erroneously attributed to a summer's run at grass.

Q. At what period of the summer may the bot-fly be expected to lay its eggs?
A. At any time between the end of June and the middle or end of September.

Q. What do the eggs look like?
A. Small hay-seeds, and I have frequently been told by farmers and even horse-dealers, that they *were* hay-seeds, until they have been convinced to the contrary.

Q. Whereabouts do the flies fix their eggs?
A. Mostly about the inside of the knees and forearms, but also along the ribs (especially the girth place), and often on the shoulders and neck. They are invariably placed at the spots where a horse can easily reach to rub and bite himself with his teeth; or where another, performing that friendly operation, is most likely to come in contact with them.

Q. Do they adhere firmly to the hair?
A. Very firmly indeed, and are difficult to get off. They may be sponged over with a weak solution of methylated spirits, or something similar, which will dry up the egg and destroy its vitality; but unless each crop of eggs is removed it is impossible to tell when fresh ones are laid amongst the old ones. A quick way of

14

removing them is to run a lighted taper over them, but this method cannot be continually repeated, and the animals should be methodically examined morning and evening, and every egg removed. It is a troublesome job, but an effectual one. The eggs can be pretty quickly removed by the aid of a sharp pen-knife.

After being swallowed the egg turns into a kind of grub, which takes up its abode in the stomach, and buries its head in the coat, where it fixes itself by the aid of two hooklets. It remains there till full-grown, occasionally perforating the stomach and thereby killing the horse ; but except for this bots are not dangerous to life, though the horse frequently becomes emaciated in the spring, from the effects of their presence. When full grown they are about the size of a blackberry, and pass naturally away during the months of June and July, when they burrow in the ground until it is time for them to become flies; then they lay their eggs, and their cycle is complete. The writer once noted eighty-four pass from a horse he bought at auction in the autumn, and whose condition rapidly fell off in the following spring, in a manner quite unaccountable until the presence of these parasites was revealed, after which the horse rapidly regained his health, and never looked back again. It is often the presence of bots internally that causes two-year-old race-horses to lose their form as the summer progresses, after showing great promise when first tried in the winter months.

Q. How is it that the parent fly is able to lay its eggs without alarming the animal during the process ?

A. The bot-fly, which is nearly as large as a honey-bee, hovers close to the spot it has selected for laying its eggs, and suspends itself perfectly motionless in the air except for the marvellous rapid vibrations of the wings, which, however, emit not the slightest hum or other sound. It then darts close to the place, its motions very much resembling those of the humming-bird moth, and suddenly extending a very long mobile ovidepositor, it curls this round in front of it, just touches the horse, and thus the egg is laid and fixed, the fly maintaining the while a perpendicular position. This operation is continued time after time until a considerable batch of eggs has been deposited.

Q. How should horses be got into condition for hunting, when coming off grass ?

A. They must not have full feeds of oats at the beginning ; and should have two bran mashes a week, to counteract the effect of the dry, concentrated food in the place of the luscious, soft grass they have been accustomed to. In a few days they should have a dose of physic ; and in about three weeks' time will require another, the indication being whether all the legs fill after work. Physic should be given in the morning, when the horse is still fasting, and he should get bran mashes for at least two nights previously. As soon as a horse has had physic administered he must have no hay and corn, and should be muzzled, or kept racked up, until his appetite begins to sicken from the medicine, lest he should eat his bedding. If this precaution is not taken, a stoppage of the bowels may ensue with serious inflammation. Balls are now made up in gelatine capsules, which make them far easier to administer than when done up in a paper covering, while the drugs retain their strength for an indefinite time.

Q.   What exercise do hunters require ?
A.   Beginning with about an hour, for a few days, they should increase to two hours, and occasionally three or four hours, as the condition improves.   At first only walking and trotting is required, but then cantering should be added, and steady gallops of two miles or more towards the end of the time.   As soon as the ground is soft enough the horses should go out cub-hunting, but it is a risk to do so when the ground is hard, for fresh horses are apt to jump about, and may easily lame themselves.   It must be borne in mind that it is long continued, slow work that throws up muscle, while the wind can only be got in order by galloping.

Q. About how long before the horses are likely to begin hunting should they be put into work ?
A.   About three months.

Q. How much exercise should horses have, when being regularly hunted ?
A.   As a general rule about two hours' slow trotting, and walking daily.   On the day after hunting a horse should not be left in the stable, if sound, but should be taken out for half an hour to an hour, to get rid of stiffness and restore the circulation.

Q.   When should hunters be fed and watered ?
A.   Where it is feasible water should be always left with the horses day and night, only being

taken away as soon as the stable is opened on a hunting morning, and not replaced until the horse has had his gruel on returning.

It is a *Golden Rule* always to " Give Water Before Feeding," and " Never Immediately After a Horse has Fed." The reverse of this is a common cause of gripes, and other internal troubles. The reason of this is that a horse has no true stomach like most other animals, but has ninety feet of intestines, the upper part being considerably larger than the lower, and as the digestion chiefly takes place while the food is passing through the large gut, it is common to speak of this as the stomach. When water is swallowed it passes rapidly through this upper portion, and if the gut should be filled at the time with a quantity of half, or totally undigested food, this is washed into the lower gut before it is in a fit state to be received there, and hence trouble ensues.

Hunters are generally fed with corn three times in the twenty-four hours, but some feeders divide the corn feeds instead into four. With delicate animals this is no doubt the better plan, for it is the nature of the horse to be feeding during the greater part of the twenty-four hours, less food is taken at one time, and the periods of waiting for food are reduced.

For horses that bolt their oats without sufficiently chewing them—as can easily be found out by observing the droppings—the oats should always be crushed, and this plan is preferable for all horses, the drawback being the greatly increased labour required. Oats when crushed should not be kept too long, as they sooner get musty than whole oats. Chopped hay also is better than long hay, and goes further, there not being so much waste ; but in small stables it is not always that the requisite labour can be spared for frequent crushing and chopping, and if this is the case it is better not attempted at all. Neither oats nor hay must be new, which the evacuations will speedily disclose, but if well harvested both may be used after the beginning of the New Year. The evacuations are sure guides to the state of health. If they are too light, or too dark in colour, probably the hay is in fault, and may be musty or bad. New hay, or oats, makes them very loose, and watery. If they are not "balled," and are offensive, the digestion is out of order, and should be at once attended to, bran mashes and bicarbonate of soda being a safe remedy ; the latter being changed for flowers of sulphur after two or three doses, mixed in the mashes. When there is no glaze on fresh droppings, and they appear instead dull and clayey, at once administer sulphate of magnesia (Epsom salts), as the indications betoken the liver is out of order, and if taken in time further trouble may be averted.

Oats should never be left long in the manger after feeding in the daytime, and half an hour afterwards any corn that has not been finished up should be removed. Nothing sickens a delicate feeder more than having oats always in the manger ; and if the horse knows the remaining ones will be taken away, it is much more apt to make an effort to consume them. It is different with the last feed at night, for many horses, especially nervous ones, will feed when all is quiet at night, which eat very sparingly in the daytime. Such horses may often with advantage have two feeds left in the mangers which they will entirely finish before morning. So long as sufficient food is taken in the twenty-four hours, it does not always do to consider too curiously when it was eaten. Though it may not be the way one would have chosen, it is better to coax an animal to eat its food somehow than go without it.

Suitable hours for feeding and exercise, for hunters, are as follows, when horses are exercised in the early morning :—

5.30. a.m.	A few mouthfuls of water (if it is not always present).
	Half the feed of oats.
	As soon as the corn is finished, exercise follows.
8 a.m.	On return give as much warmed water as the horses will drink.
	Then the rest of the feed of oats and
	Hay.
11 to 12 o'clock according to the time the horses were fed after exercise.	Feed of oats.
4 o'clock.	Water.
4 to 6 o'clock.	Oats
	Then hay.

Horses that are not exercised till late in the day will have their full feed of oats the first thing instead of dividing it.

Horses going to hunt will have no hay in the morning, but instead have another double handful of oats at 8 a.m.

Delicate feeders have a double quantity of oats at 6 p.m. ; or get an additional feed at 8 p.m.

Horses vary considerably in the amount they

consume, but hunters should eat from 12 to 14 lbs. of oats per day, and about 11 lbs. of hay. If more oats are consumed, less hay will be eaten, and *vice versâ*.

A feed of oats is roughly a quartern measure, the fourth part of a peck. A peck is the fourth part of a bushel ; and four bushels should go to a sack.

Oats are now sold by the weight, which alteration from selling by measure arose from the Railway Companies only recognising weight in their transactions.

```
1 ton      ...      ... = 20 cwt. = 160 stone = 2,240 lbs.
1 quarter of oats = 2 sacks =  24 stone
1 sack ...      ...      ...      =  12 stone
1 truss of straw      ...      =  28 lbs.
1 truss of old meadow-hay  =  56 lbs.
```

1 sack of oats, allowing 12 lbs. per diem, lasts a horse 14 days
1 truss of hay   ,,   11 lbs.   ,,   ,,   ,,   5 ,,
2 trusses straw   ,,   ,,   ,,   ,,   ,,   5 ,,
    1 ton of hay should last 6 horses 1 month.

Oats should feel heavy when weighed in the hand, and have plenty ofi kernel in comparison to the husk. A thick-skinned variety may look larger until the grain is extracted, and the latter then found smaller than the thinner skinned oat. Black oats have less husk than white ones. Oats should be free from any musty smell, and if kept in bulk must be frequently turned over to allow air to circulate round them. If kept in a very confined place it is sometimes convenient to put them in sacks, and constantly reverse the position of each, but they keep better when freely exposed. Oats are fit to use when the grain divides clean and sharp when bitten between the teeth.

Quite as important as oats, if indeed not more

so, is the quality of the hay supplied to horses doing fast work. A diversity of opinion exists as to whether old meadow, or clover hay is the better, but in meadow-hay there is a greater variety of herbage, which should be an advantage. It should be grown on up-land, and the important part is that the grass should be cut when still full of sap, before it has ripened into woody fibre, and that the weather conditions should be suitable for making it. If there is plenty of sun, a moderate amount of wind, an absence of rain, and the hay is put into stack so that it will sweat just enough, and not too much, the hay should remain a green colour, with a sweet aromatic odour. On such hay horses will thrive heartily, and they eat it with avidity. If not enough sweated hay is soft to handle, and horses do not care for it; while if too much sweated, and dark in colour, with the scent of Cavendish tobacco, though horses will eat it greedily, it is not good for their digestions. If stacked when wet there will be mouldly streaks, which may affect the hay for a considerable distance, and which is both distasteful to the horses and prejudicial.

Meadow-hay should consist of the finest grasses with but few of the tall, coarse ones in it, which are more suitable for cows than horses. It should be full of clover, sweet vernal, crested dogstail, and perennial rye-grass, with foxtail, timothy, and yarrow. The cock's-foot does not make good hay for horses, being too coarse, though it affords a valuable bite in the spring, growing before the others. The " barometer " of the haymaker is the crested dogstail, and when that comes into flower is the time to cut the grass —if the weather is fine. All the grasses flower in regular rotation, the crested dogstail being about the middle, so that if the meadow is cut when this grass is fully in flower, the earlier grasses have not yet begun to seed—when woody fibre begins to form—while the later grasses are just coming into flower, and therefore will not produce more herbage. No herb makes any more growth when once the flowering process is commenced.

Delicate feeders may be further tempted by having a double-handful (about 1 lb.) of crushed oil-cake, malt, or barley mixed with their corn ; and a horse that is not thriving is often benefited by having a wine-glassful of linseed oil poured daily into the oats, which should then be stirred up until they have absorbed the oil, which they will quickly do. Often plenty of carrots—a bucketful a day—will change a starved-looking, unthrifty horse into a round, muscular, handsome animal, that its owner can scarcely recognise. Rock-salt should always be in each manger, for nothing is more conducive to health than a plentiful supply of salt.

A horse that is recovering from an illness should always have a tonic for a short time ; and also one that is losing flesh with its work. The tonics usually employed are gentian and camomile to promote appetite; sulphate of iron, or Fowler's solution of arsenic (Liquor Arsenicalis), to redden the blood ; and powdered ginger to give tone to the stomach. By turning up the lips and looking at the gums, it can be seen whether the red corpuscles are deficient in the blood, which will be indicated by the pale, almost white appearance of the gums. Arsenic is a most valuable remedy, but requires care in

its administration, for it is an accumulative
poison, and is the constant source of poisoning
horses, when administered by grooms and carters
to give brilliance to the coats of their charges. A
dose, harmless in itself, may, if long continued,
prove in the end a fatal one, for as the addition
of another drop to an already full tea-cup causes
it to overflow, so the giving of one more dose to
an animal, in whose system the arsenic has
accumulated to the utmost limit it can stand, is a
cause of immediate death. The law courts can
give proof of this, in which juries have not
always been skilfully directed ; and one celebrated murder case may recur to the minds of
some, in which the conviction that followed
might never have occurred, had the jury been
composed of men accustomed to the use of this
drug amongst horses, and been familiar with its
peculiar effects. To be quite safe, it is better not
to administer it for more than a fortnight at a
time, with at least a similar interval before
recommencing ; the dose recommended is thirty
drops. It should never be administered at the
same time as **physic** ; nor should it be used at
any time if the bowels are in a loose state.

Sometimes when horses are out at grass they
obtain access to yew with fatal effect, though at
other times they seem to eat it with impunity.
Undoubtedly it is most dangerous when half-
withered, such as yew-clippings, or twigs that
have been caught by a frost, and died. The
symptoms are those of narcotic poisoning, with
fits of shivering and coldness of the skin.

The treatment to be adopted should consist of
purgatives to get rid of the poison, and stimulants
to combat the general prostration.

The *Veterinarian* published a few years ago the following treatment, which had been proved successful for cattle, and the same method should prove also suitable for horses :—

YEW POISONING.

Solution of Aloes	...	...	... 3 oz.
Nitric Ether	...	...	... 1 oz.
Tincture of Opium	...	...	... 1 oz.
Aromatic Spirit of Ammonia		...	½ oz.
Linseed Tea	...	...	... 1 pint.

If necessary the dose may be repeated, without the aloes and opium, every three or four hours.

The symptoms of a common cold are only too well known, but they usually yield to simple treatment. Do not give drastic purgatives, or strong sedatives, but rather saline draughts ; and as soon as thick discharge commences to flow from the nostrils, vegetable tonics may be given ; and later sulphate of iron will assist recovery.

Belladonna has a great effect, and ten drops of the Vet. Homeopathic Tincture, twice a day, is excellent. If the glands are swollen behind the jaws, or under them, mustard may be rubbed over them, and washed off in ten minutes ; or the following liniment may be applied :—

Saponis Mollis	...	...	... iv. oz.
Camphor	...	...	... ii. oz.
Liq. Ammon. Fortis.		...	... iii. oz.
Spt. Vini Recti	...	...	... xvi. oz.

The food should consist of bran-mashes with linseed gruel, and water with the chill off ; and when recovering " boiled oats," turnips, carrots, and green food if obtainable. " Boiled oats " are made by mixing up the bran and oats together in a bucket, and after pouring in boiling linseed gruel, or water, stirring the whole well up, and then covering over with a horse-cloth until the whole is cool enough to be partaken of.

In the drinking water should be placed three times daily—

Sulph. Magnes.	...	...	...	3⅕ oz.
Pulv. Potash Nit.	...	...	...	3⅕ drachm.

Water should always be present with a sick horse.

If much prostration should prevail, with fever, give—

Nitric Ether	...	...	...	1 to 2 oz.
Water	...	...	...	1 pint,

every three or four hours.

If the prostration increases give in addition every twelve hours—

Nitrate Potassæ	...	...	2 drachms.
Gentian ...	...	...	2 ,,
Powd. Ginger ...	...	...	2 ,,

Strangles, which so often attack a young horse on first coming into a stable, require the same treatment, only the glands will require poulticing and lancing, if they do not at once become reduced after the application of the mustard, or liniment.

Colic is a very common ailment. It may be distinguished from inflammation of the intestines in that in the former case the attacks of griping pains are intermittent, while in inflammation they are continuous.

For colic administer—

Bicarb. Soda	...	...	...	2 drachms.
Tinct. of Ginger		...	...	1½ oz.

mixed in a pint of lukewarm water.
For cases of great pain add—

Tinct. of Opium		...	...	...	1 oz. ;

or the following may be substituted :—

Tinct. Cinnabis Indica		...	...	ii. oz.
Mucilag. Acacia	...	...	...	iv. oz.
Aquæ Menth. Pipert.	...	...	...	viii. oz.

Administer the dose, and if the pain does not subside give another half-dose.

If the colic should proceed from drinking water, such as changing from soft to hard water (which used very commonly to attack horses at Gibraltar that had lately arrived), 10 drops of the Homœopathic Vet. Tinct. Aconite should be administered instead, and repeated every 15 or 20 minutes, until relief is obtained.

In a case of diarrhœa water should be removed, and withheld, and no oats, bran mashes, or hay should be allowed ; but a little dry bran may be given at first, followed by bran made just moist. If the attack continues, give a drench of 1 tea-cup-ful of starch well dissolved in a quart of warm water, with 60 drops of laudanum. If great weakness should set in, give a bottle of port wine. The following prescription should be given at once, and repeated 3 or 4 times per day if necessary :—

Prepared Chalk	...	...	...	2 drachms.
Ginger	...	...	...	2 ,,
Ol. Pep.	...	...	...	10 to 15 drops.

If there is much pain add—

Tinct. of Opium ... ... 1 oz.

In case of great distress after hunting, administer—

Magnes. Sulph. ... ... iv. oz.
Pulv. Pot. Nit. ... ... iv. drachms.
Water ... ... 1 pint.
and add 2 glasses of gin or whisky.

Choking.—At the back of the mouth are situated the openings of the œsophagus and windpipe. The upper one communicates with the stomach, and the lower one with the lungs. If the obstruction that causes choking is situated in the œsophagus, gentle pressure may be tried, and a little linseed oil poured down ; but in giving the latter great care must be taken not to hold the head up by force, or some of the oil may find its way down the windpipe, and into the lungs, thus choking the horse. If any oil is forced back, it will probably have to return through the nostrils.

Mud-fever is a rash, which frequently occurs from a chill, usually from perspiration being suddenly checked, as from standing in a lane after a sharp gallop, with a cold wind playing upon one side. It most generally attacks horses when only half fit.

Give

Sulph. Magnes. ... ... 2 oz.
Common Salt ... ... ½ oz.

in a mash for two or three nights ; to be followed by

Liquor Arsenicalis ... ... 30 drops

twice a day for a fortnight.

If the spots become irritable, or sore, they may be treated with

| Glycerine | ... | ... | ... | 1 part. |
| Water | ... | ... | ... | 15 to 20 parts, |

or apply zinc ointment.

For worms give :—

To a foal on the mare { Linseed Oil, $\frac{1}{4}$ pint.
Turpentine, $\frac{1}{2}$ tablespoon

To a yearling   ... { Linseed Oil, $\frac{1}{2}$ pint.
Turpentine, 1 tablespoon.

To a full-grown horse { Linseed Oil, $\frac{1}{2}$ pint.
Turpentine, 1 oz. (2 tablespoons.)
Camphor, $\frac{1}{2}$ oz.

The camphor should be put in the oil in the evening, when it will be dissolved by the next morning.

The success of the treatment very much depends upon the complete fasting of the animal for twenty-four hours previous to the administration of the dose.

Tonic after illness :

Powd. Gentian ...	...	...	1 drachm.
,, Camomile	...	...	1 drachm.
,, Ginger ...	...	...	1 drachm.
,, Sulph. Iron	...	...	2 drachms.

To be given daily, mixed with a feed of oats, for a week or fortnight.

When the liver is out of order, the animal showing yellowish eyes, skin, and gums, give morning and evening for 4 days in the drinking water

| Magnes. Sulph. | ... | ... | ... | iv. oz. |
| Pulv. Pot. Nit. | ... | ... | ... | iii. drachms. |

One of the advantages of turning horses out to grass, especially after they have been ill, and have reached the convalescent stage, is that they are enabled to swallow some earth, which is necessary for the due regulation of the stomach, and the want of which is a frequent cause of indigestion : but care must be taken that it is not of a gritty, sandy nature, which is of itself prejudicial.

It used to be annoying to see an animal, when it was allowed to have its head loose for a few minutes in order to pick a little sweet grass, proceed instead to take several bites of earth, filling its mouth full, raising its nose in the air, and champing it with most evident satisfaction until the saliva and mud trickled out of its mouth. At length it dawned upon me that the horse did so because it felt the want of it ; and then it soon became self-evident that when at grass a horse must pick up a certain amount of earth, when close grazing. The notion being once started, further observation soon confirmed the truth of it ; and it is almost invariably the case that any horse which has been long stabled will prefer, when he first gets the chance, to take some mouthfuls of mud rather than the sweetest grass, if he has long been without the coveted morsel. In further illustration of this, Speculum, formerly the famous sire at Moorlands, used to suffer much from indigestion, until the idea was formed of giving him some chalk to nibble at ; and for the later years of his life he was invariably supplied with this luxury, with much benefit to his health.

It was interesting to find, when racing in Spain, that here, too, was the same notion, and that a favourite remedy for indigestion was to cook up a mess of chalk, like porridge, and add it to a bran mash. In this case, as in most others, the proof of the pudding was in the eating.

For this reason, when giving carrots in the winter time, it is as well not to have them washed too clean, unless they have been grown on a sandy soil, for sand is apt to cause indigestion.

In England many articles of food are neglected, that are much valued elsewhere, and an excellent " salad " for horses is too often cast aside—the green-tops, and outer stalks of celery, of which horses get inordinately fond when once they have acquired a taste for them. Other items, too, are chicory leaves, dandelions, and watercress, all of which are most valuable blood-purifiers, when first they push their leaves in the spring.

A very good physic ball is composed of—

Aloes	...	...	...	3 to 4 drachms.
Gentian	...	...	...	2 drachms.
Ginger	...	...	...	1 drachm ;

the addition of these last two ingredients being a powerful factor in preventing griping. The balls should be enveloped in gelatine capsules.

If a horse does not feed well after the physic is " set," give in a pint of warm water :

Gentian ...	...	...	...	...	$\frac{1}{2}$ oz.
Nitric Ether	...	...	...	...	$\frac{1}{2}$ oz.

Excellent alterative powders, especially for a horse that is debilitated, are made of—

Flower of Sulphur	...	...	...	4 oz.
White Resin	...	...	...	...	,,
Black Antimony	...	...	...	,,
Prepared Nitre ...	...	...	...	,,

a tablespoonful to be given in a mash for twenty-one nights, and every fourth morning half a pint of pure linseed oil administered as a drench.

Every one should be able to feel a horse's pulse, which is most conveniently felt where the artery passes over the under jaw at the bottom of the cheek. It may range from 34 to 42 beats per minute. This with the respirations from 8 to 12 per minute, is generally correct, but it is subject to variation from the surrounding temperatures of the stable, and of the animal, and whether before or after feeding.

The temperature of the horse ranges in health from 100 to 101, the former being most usual; but if all other indications point to good health, such variation of temperature may be accepted as normal.

An artery is sometimes severed out hunting, and the general course of them should be studied, to be able to apply pressure by a makeshift tourniquet, until a clot of blood has formed, and the bleeding stopped. If no one is able to perform this office, the horse may easily bleed to death, when it could otherwise be saved. The writer has occasionally used dry grass twisted into lumps, or a smooth pebble wrapped in a handker-chief, utilising a latch-key, pocket-knife, or bit of stick from the nearest hedge, to tighten the make-shift bandage and by twisting it to hold it in its place; the two ends of the handkerchief should be knotted together after they have been placed round the leg. On two occasions when the facial artery had burst it was easy to keep the bandage in its place by adjusting the noseband so that it could be strapped tightly over the injury.

Hunters are apt to get staked in the abdomen,

and if this should happen it may be fatal if not at once attended to, though if the intestines themselves are not injured, the protruding portion may be pushed back, and if the hole in the wall of the abdomen is only small, it may possibly be closed by inserting a safety-pin through the lips of the skin ; or by pushing a long pin through, and then twisting anything round the two ends in a figure of 8, to keep the pin in its place. If dirt has got into the wound or clings to the intestine, it should be carefully wiped off before the gut is returned, and, of course, professional assistance must be obtained at the earliest opportunity.

A little knowledge is apt to be a dangerous thing. Some years ago the writer happened to be standing at the second last fence at a fashionable meeting near London when a horse fell, and not getting up at once was immediately surrounded by a crowd as usual. Immediately there was a cry, " The horse has staked itself ! Send for a gun ! " and while a messenger was despatched to the stand for a weapon, others sat on the unfortunate animal's neck to prevent it rising. The crowd was so dense the writer was unable to inspect the animal, but a young gentleman, apparently two- or three-and-twenty years of age, made himself very conspicuous in the centre of the lookers-on, vociferating, " Why doesn't the gun come ? " and throwing his arms about, apparently taking the direction of everything upon himself. At last a man came running up with a gun, which the young gentleman seized from him, and while the crowd scattered on each side he pointed the weapon at the animal's forehead, and making a well-directed shot, put an end to its existence. When the crowd dispersed the

youth still remained, apparently somewhat ex-
hansted by his previous excitement, and as there
was now an opportunity of seeing what injury
had really been sustained, the writer carefully
examined the dead animal. There was one tiny
hole in the abdomen, and from it protruded a
minute portion of intestine about the size of a
walnut ; and the closest investigation did not
disclose any injury whatever to the gut at all.
The youth looked on while the examination was
being made, and at the close of it the writer stood
up, and addressing him, said, "You are a veterinary
surgeon, I presume, sir?" "Nothing of the
sort," he replied with a haughty air. "But,"
was the rejoinder, "you ordered the horse to be
shot." "Of course I did," he answered, "why,
it was staked!" "There was nothing the matter
there that the horse would not have recovered
from in ten days," said the writer, "and it might
have been running again here at the next meeting." "But it was *staked!*" replied the youth,
with great emphasis, as though that statement
admitted of no argument. "If I was the owner
of the horse," was the answer, "I should certainly
bring an action against you for the unwarrantable
destruction of my property." The youth waited
to hear no more, and turning round fled towards
the stand as fast as he could run.

In all cases of punctures of the skin it is necessary to close the opening immediately by the
means mentioned above, in order to prevent air
from entering the wound, which would otherwise pass under the skin, blowing it out like a
bladder during the journey home, and producing
a curious feeling of crackling when the hand is
passed over the skin. When the opening is very

large and the means for closing it are inadequate, a handkerchief or something similar should be stuffed into the wound to close it, until professional help can be obtained. In all such cases it is well to give a dose of aconite as soon as possible, either the Homœopathic Vet. Tincture (a dose of any Homœopathic Vet. Preparation is invariably 10 drops, mixed with a little water), or the Allopathic, whichever can be obtained. Aconite has a powerful effect in controlling fever.

Of all ailments to which hunters are liable, that of lameness is necessarily the most common, from the "rough and tumble" nature of their arduous work. It is often a difficult matter to say where the cause of lameness is seated, and a few hints on this subject may be useful.

The first thing to settle is which leg is the lame one; and secondly what part of that limb is affected. Then by careful examination the actual place will usually be discovered, though often inflammation and swelling, and consequent tenderness, is so diffused that the precise spot cannot always be fixed upon at first with certainty.

Q. When a horse is lame on a fore-leg, how can this be determined?

A. By standing in front of the horse as it is trotted towards you, and watching which knee is bent as the head droops. This is the lame leg.

Q. How is lameness in a hind-leg detected?

A. By standing behind the horse as it is trotted away from you, and noticing which hip is raised with a jerk, higher than the other. This hind-leg is the lame one. If the hock is raised as high as the other the lameness is below the hock, and *vice versâ*. In the latter case there is first a droop of the hip until the foot is about to be placed on the ground, when it is jerked upward.

Q. Does it matter on what sort of ground the horse is trotted?

A. The horse should first be trotted on hard ground on the level, and then on soft ground if necessary. It may further be trotted up, and then down an incline, to help a decision to be made in obscure cases.

Q. What is learned from these different methods?

A. A horse that is slightly lame on account of a splint forming, or in the foot, will show unevenness in action on hard ground, such as a road, but may go nearly, if not quite sound, when trotted on soft turf. On the other hand, horses lame from muscular ailments, or when the tendons or joints are affected, go quite as lame in deep as on hard ground, even if not more so.

A horse lame in front may trot almost sound uphill, and go proppy at once when coming down an incline ; while the contrary is the case when the lameness is behind.

The first thing to do, before having the horse trotted, is to visit it in the stable when in a state of rest, and observe the position in which it stands. Grooms too frequently give a horse a slap with the hand, and then take hold of its head-collar and move the animal when a visitor approaches, wishing to try and make it look its best; if such a thing should happen, wait a few minutes and engage in conversation until the horse relapses again into its normal state, observing it keenly all the time.

Horses often rest their legs when standing, but if they advance a fore-leg they almost always have the opposite hind-leg advanced also if they are sound, and no notice need be taken of this. If a fore-leg only is pointed forward, however, it is generally a sign of trouble somewhere, probably in the foot, and a careful examination should be made. A hind-leg is often alone flexed when the horse is only resting, and in all probability it will shortly shift its weight on to that leg and rest the other.

When the tendons are strained the horse flexes the leg, and there is no difficulty in diagnosing this case, for the heat, swelling, and tenderness shown on pressure being applied, indicate at once where the mischief lies. In navicular the leg is also flexed, but usually only the fetlock, the knee-joint being straightened, while the weight is borne by the toe, the heel being slightly raised off the ground. A further test may be applied by bending the foot up as much as possible, and applying pressure to the heel with the thumb.

Navicular lameness may be distinguished from rheumatism in the shoulder when the horse is in action, for with rheumatism he only gets worse the longer he is out; while with navicular he gets better as he gets warm, until he may appear quite sound. With rheumatism he usually walks lame, but with navicular he may walk sound, and trot lame. The muscles of the shoulder frequently waste with rheumatism, and this is best detected when standing in front and facing the horse.

Acute laminitis is indicated by great heat in the foot, which frequently extends high up the leg, and may throw the inquirer off the right scent. The almost total inability of the horse to move should, however, prevent any mistake being made. The treatment recommended has been mentioned on a previous page.

Chronic laminitis is shown by loss of the concave form of the sole, by wavy circular ridges in the hoofs, by an abnormal degree of heat in the foot, and by the animal treading as much as possible on his heels, especially in the trot. A lame leg does not cover so much ground in its stride as a sound one, and the extent to which the hind-foot covers the print of the fore-foot must be carefully watched. Horses, however, that have been hunted by ladies throughout the season almost invariably walk much shorter with the off hind-foot than with the near one, and yet go sound when put into a trot. This arises from the pressure thrown on the off-side of the withers, by the lady's weight being supported chiefly by the stirrup and crutch on the near side ; and to accommodate himself to this, the horse shortens his stride on the off-side.

If a fore-leg is lame the corresponding hind-foot will cover the print of the fore-foot, when walking to a greater extent than the other hind-foot covers its fore-print, for the strides of the two hind-legs are equal (except as above), while those of the two fore-legs are unequal.

In the case of the lameness of the hind-leg the contrary is the case, the strides of the two hind-legs being unequal, while those of the fore-legs are equal. The sound hind-leg, therefore, covers its fore-print to a greater extent than its fellow lame one does, as the power to bring forward the lame hind-leg is necessarily deficient.

Q. When examining a horse for soundness, what methods should be used?

A. After trotting and walking the horse to see if it is sound it is usual to begin with the head, and after examining the eyes, and the glands of the neck and under the jaws, to glance over the neck to see if there are any signs of having been bled at any time. The hand is then run over each leg in succession; and finally the horse is tested for wind. If it can be ridden it must be sent along at a gallop for some distance, and only pulled up when close to the examiner, so that he may hear the breathing when fully developed. The horse should then be threatened with a stick to see if it grunts; turned round sharply each way in a circle of its own length to test for string-halt; and finally backed to see if it is a " shiverer." If any doubt as to lameness exists, the horse should be put into a stable for at least half an hour, and then led out again. While if there is the least suspicion of broken wind a man should be put on the horse's bare back, without a saddle, when evidence of the malady will at once be given which may have escaped every other test.

Q. What is a " shiverer "?
A. It is a nervous disease connected with paralysis, and quite incurable. The animal may look perfectly well and move all right when going straight forward, but it cannot go backwards. The horse is useless for work, except of the slightest description.

Q. Can horses be prevented from kicking in the stable?

A. Eighteen inches of a light chain attached to a broad felt-lined strap, which is buckled above the hind fetlock, is often effectual, as the horse hits himself when he commences to kick.

If this plan fails a strong, leather, felt-lined strap should be buckled above each hind fetlock, with a strong, short chain connecting the two straps. The horse can lie down and get up without difficulty, but he cannot kick with either leg.

Q. If a horse is apt to bite when being dressed, how should he be treated?

A. Much depends upon the man who grooms it; but if he cannot manage the animal otherwise it may either be racked up, or muzzled, or a wooden bit put in his mouth, the latter being made the thickness of a stable-fork, or a sidestick fastened to the head-collar, and roller (which must be worn) which is changed to either side of the horse as required.

Q. Can any treatment be suggested for wind-suckers?

A. In some cases a broad strap round the throat is effectual, the drawback to it being the wearing away of the mane behind the ears. A triangular piece of metal encased in leather is often attached, which projects into the angle between the jaws, and hinders the horse from arching his neck to suck in the wind.

In determined cases the surest preventative is a hollow bit open at both ends with numerous holes in the front side, so that when the horse sucks in the air it escapes through the open ends. The bit must be worn constantly except when feeding, and continual care must be exercised to see that the bit is kept clean and does not get plugged up, and that the holes are all open. By filling his stomach with air the wind-sucker brings on a violent form of colic, with much pain. The belly is greatly distended, and should be gently hand-rubbed.

Give at once—

Arom. Spts. Ammonia	...	...	$\frac{1}{2}$ oz.
Powd. Ginger	...	...	...	$\frac{1}{2}$ oz.
Warm Water...	...	...	...	1 pint.

The ammonia to be added the last thing.
To be repeated in twenty minutes.

Q. Do not horses sometimes injure their hips when entering or leaving the stable ?

A. Yes, many a horse gets a " hip down " ; that is, chips off the prominent bone of the hip, through a careless attendant allowing it to collide with the doorpost. Some horses are awkward about entering the stable, due very often to some former accident when doing so, and after hesitating make a rush through the doorway. Such animals are very liable to an accident. If a horse does not come quietly the bridle-rein should be lowered instead of pulled at, and the groom should precede but not look the horse in the face, and endeavour to coax it to follow. The precaution of lowering the bridle-rein is very necessary when entering a low stable door, for if pulled at the horse will probably throw up its head, and may seriously injure its poll.

CHAPTER IX

RIDING TO HOUNDS

In England only a small proportion of those gathered together at the meet attempt to follow in the wake of the hounds, the remainder usually galloping helter-skelter through the nearest gate, and down a friendly lane ; or else crawling cautiously through the gaps made by the bolder spirits who are vanishing in the distance. In Ireland, on the contrary, a stranger from this side of the Channel, making his first acquaintance with an Irish pack, is surprised to see how every one of the heterogeneous gathering at the covert-side, men, maids, and children, from the oldest to the youngest, do their utmost to follow the hounds to the best of their ability and the capacity of their steeds. The general absence of convenient roads, and the fact that if there should be such an unusual thing as a gate out of a field, it is sure to be an iron one, securely fastened with padlock and chain to stone gate-posts, may perhaps account for this feature of an Irish hunt. Anyhow, the moment the pack leaves the covert, away every one follows in pursuit ; and such obstacles as probably the Saxon has never seen in his own country—walls, banks, ditches, and boggy or rough ground—are all successfully surmounted, though they may at first cause many qualms to any one inexperienced in such a chase.

The chief pleasure in taking leaps has always seemed to be the sensation imparted of flying; and this is scarcely experienced to the same degree when jumping banks as in taking flying-fences. The triumphant feeling of having surmounted difficulties is, however, the same in either case; and this is often as conspicuous when successfully traversing intricate mountain sides, with insecure foothold, as in more level and cultivated countries. All call for readiness of resource, and a steadiness of nerve, that are invaluable for testing manly qualities. It matters little in what country the scene is laid, the thrill is the same that permeates the right sort when a view-holloa proclaims that the fox is away, whether the country that lies before them is over flying-fences, banks, or rough moors; and the only question that then arises in their minds is whether they are about to be blessed with a really good scent, with a reasonable hope of a glorious gallop.

After a young horse of the right conformation and action, with plenty of speed, has been procured either by purchase, or, what is still more satisfactory, been bred from the old mare, the first important stage in its education is teaching it to jump. Unless the animal can take its fences with steadiness and due care, it will never become a first-class hunter.

There is a right way, and a wrong way of doing everything, and as so much depends upon the earliest lessons with a horse, with its marvellously retentive memory, it is most essential that the right way should be pursued from the very commencement. In this the teaching of Ireland, that grand nursery of young hunters, may well be followed. A horse there learns to jump banks, ditches, and all kinds of obstacles without any weight on its back, being led over them with a long rope until it understands thoroughly what is required of it, and not till then is it asked to jump with a person on its back. How different is this from the ordinary way in England, where usually a man endeavours to ride the young horse over small places, following the lead of another, before the pupil knows at all how to make its spring ; and when any scramble that ensues is much aggravated by the clumsiness and weight of the rider. The latter, too, is frequently nervous ; and his tremors are at once communicated to the animal, in that mysterious way whereby it so quickly divines the thoughts of the man on its back.

In the early lessons it is most important that the pupil should be thoroughly imbued with the notion that timber is not to be broken ; and the bar over which it commences to jump should be so strong that a fall, or at least a great struggle to prevent one, is the certain result of taking liberties with it. The bar should be kept quite low at first, not higher than the animal's knees, indeed, and only gradually raised. It should never be put to a good height until the young horse has hit it once or twice, and learned how to save a fall, for if this does not happen till the bar is a really good height, the pupil does not know what is going to happen when he makes a mistake, and may break a fore-leg, by not being prepared for the weight that will come upon it.

It is well to visit other packs occasionally, though a practice of constantly selecting good meets with them sometimes ends in mortification, from missing a good run with your own pack and having a bad day with the one selected. He who sticks to his own hounds, taking the favourite and the unfashionable fixtures as they come, is almost sure to be in " the good thing " when it does come off, and often this occurs when least expected. Though if the huntsman of your own pack has unfortunately proved himself incompetent, and the neighbouring huntsman is a genius, it can scarcely be expected that any one should sacrifice his season for the sake of being a martyr to principle !

A first-rate rider to hounds must be possessed of many natural gifts, that surely some good fairy must bestow on him at his birth, and it is no doubt owing to the rarity of their all being combined in one individual, that so few attain to the position of being able to take their own line, and hold their place to the end of a really fine gallop. Many a good man can take his own line, so long as there is some one else alongside, or slightly in front, who insensibly maps out the direction to be followed, and who is gifted with that eye to hounds which is so rare. But supposing the fugleman comes to grief, or drops back from the inability of his horse to sustain the pressure of the pace, the other resembles a ship without a rudder, and loses sight and touch of the pack within two or three fields. It is not always from want of nerve or decision, but rather from not having an intuitive knowledge of what the fox—and hence the hounds—is likely to do under any given circumstances, that the rider is thrown out when left to his own resources; and he also fails to notice, and appraise at their right value, all such movements on the part of birds and beasts, met with in the course of the gallop, which would at once have given a clue to the other, if only he had still been there to make the running. To gather up all these threads when going at racing pace a man needs to have the keenest eyesight and hearing, and the gift of coming to a rapid decision; and he further requires iron nerves, a strong seat, and the best of hands, if he aspires to lead the field in a forty-minutes' run. He must have the faculty of instantly selecting a practicable way out of a field, the moment he has jumped into it, in the direction the hounds are heading. Though others at starting may be in front for a field or two, they do not remain there. Whenever the pack really settles down to run, the same leaders are certain to be in their places, at the head of a string of followers, if only they are riding horses that have the gift of going. Such men seldom take the trouble to go in front in a slow run, and are then not noticed; but should the scent change, should heads go up, and sterns go down, and the pack suddenly lengthen out as they race on a scent that gives them scant time to talk about it, all lethargy is thrown off in an instant, and the real leaders come to the front almost in the twinkling of an eye.

Many a horse that can keep his place with the hounds, if he happens to get away with them when they leave the covert, has not the requisite pace to catch up the pack if they have a start of

16

a field or two; especially is this the case if there are many riders to pass who have been more fortunately situated, and who block the way in calm content, not attempting to hurry up, and who would not be with the pack for two fields if they happened for once to find themselves with them. It is equally heart-breaking work to find oneself on a horse too slow to get to the hounds in a fast, straight gallop; or to be hampered by duffers in front, who are irretrievably causing you to lose the run. On this subject Mr. Elsey makes some pithy remarks, that have both pathos and humour in them.

"All I can say is, it is a bit awkward to find yourself in a biggish country, on a windy day, when you have got badly away, and the hounds are able to run in spite of the wind, and have not yet got more than two fields in front; and then when by sharp galloping you are getting within touch of them, you catch up three or four ladies riding hard for a line of gates, which etiquette demands you must open for them. This game has to be repeated, till a road lets you get away from them, either by jumping out of it, or galloping on, and getting up to the hounds, if only you have such luck!"

Most of us have been in such a strait, and Mr. Elsey will have the sympathy of ardent spirits, whose keenness perhaps outweighs their gallantry at such an inopportune moment, more especially since two have ever been held the right number for company! But the people who do these things, who hesitate at the only available gap, who pull up almost to a walk to go through an open gate, and who canter slowly down a narrow lane, when hounds are leaving the field

behind with a breast-high scent, have no notion
of what they are doing, for they have never
ridden up to hounds in their lives in a fast
thing ; and they are quite unconscious that they
are spoiling the sport of gallant riders behind
them, who are sadly chafing at the loss of the
opportunity which the others are incapable of
turning to account.

All authority is by unwritten law vested in
the M.F.H. for the time being, and any one
transgressing against the general interests of
those who are out, or of the Hunt in general,
must take in good part any reprimand or orders
he may receive, whether for riding too close to
the hounds, heading the fox, or any other mal-
feasance. The master, on his part, should be
sure of his ground before he finds fault with
any person, and should remember that he is as
much bound by the courtesy expected between
gentlemen as would be the case in any other
sphere.

Rough manners may be overlooked for sufficient
local reasons, but they cannot be excused ; and
are most certainly unnecessary for the due carrying on of the proceedings. If a M.F.H. cannot
keep order without bad language and much scold-
ing, he is scarcely the right man in the right
place, and will only be tolerated if the sport
shown under his *régime* is of an exceptionally
high order.

When commencing to hunt, the beginner
should make a start on a clever old hunter that
knows its business thoroughly and can take care
both of itself and its rider, for the latter cannot
possibly understand at first how each description
of fence requires to be done, and he will learn

much from such a steed. It will not matter if
it is rather a screw, so long as it is sound enough
to do its share of the partnership, the main thing
being that it is thoroughly accomplished and
easy to ride, so that the pupil may have no
difficulty in following where he sees other people
go. It is time enough to get on to a raw, or
difficult, horse when knowledge has come of
what to do and how to do it ; then it is necessary
to ride more difficult horses, for no one ever
became a really fine horseman by only riding
well-made hunters.

One of the first things to be attended to is to
see that the novice has his stirrups the right
length, which is often too much left to chance ;
for on this ultimately depends his power in the
saddle, and the possession of a seat no antics of a
horse should be able to disturb. On a strong seat
also to a great extent hinges the acquirement of
first-rate hands, for if the rider finds it necessary
to use the reins to preserve his balance, he cannot
expect his horse to be ever on the alert to obey
their slightest indication ; nor can he ride with
the long reins that are essential to perfect hands,
when he continually is obliged to steady himself
by their aid.

Ladies are generally supposed to have better
hands than most men, and possibly this is the
case ; though the best men have every bit as
delicate hands, and also more power in addition.

Of bits there are an endless variety, many
unsuitable, from their severity, for riding across
country horses with ordinary mouths. It is
most usually the rider's hands that are in fault
when a horse cannot be ridden in an ordinary

simple bit, though horses are occasionally to be found which will only go pleasantly in one particular bit, and are difficult to control with any other. Many horses have a trick of getting their tongues over the bit, which in most cases is due to carelessness in allowing the bit to hang down too low when they were first bitted; and when they do this a rider possesses very little control over them. Such horses, if determined goers, are almost unrideable unless some means are adopted of preventing them from putting this habit into practice. A horse should always be ridden in the easiest bit in which he can be controlled, and the amount of falls that are caused by bits being too severe is incalculable. They not only cause a horse to jump short, and drop his hind-legs into the ditch on the far side, but they also cause him to snatch at the bit, or toss his head up, from being afraid of being hurt, when the rider wishes to steady his horse in its gallop. Without a smooth, easy, but firm hold of the bit, it is impossible to race a horse at a big place without first pulling him out of his stride, and then setting him going again.

Saddles may be comfortable, or the reverse, and there is a great difference as to whether they are easy to remain in, or not. A plain-flapped saddle, that slopes forward, gives a horse that stops suddenly in his track, or is a determined kicker or bucker, an undue chance of getting rid of his rider. If plain flaps are preferred, there should be some stuffing underneath, that will raise the front of the flap sufficiently to prevent the leg having a tendency to slip forward, especially when going down steep hills. Stuffed flaps are easier to ride in, and give a more secure hold, as any breaker of experience will surely endorse. They also occasion less fatigue to the rider, as it is not necessary to be constantly tightening the muscles of the thighs to keep the balance. Saddles must have plenty of room between the pommel and the cantle, to allow for the rider's frame with something to spare, for it is a painful thing to alight on the cantle after a jump; and still more so, and withal dangerous, to come down on the pommel. A point also that should be attended to is that the saddle be made wide enough, for a narrow saddle is uncomfortable for the rider, and does not sufficiently distribute the weight on the horse's back, putting it too much in one place. The flap should be carried well back towards the cantle, for if the angle it makes at its junction with the seat comes just under the rider's thigh it will continually ruck up the breeches into a crease, which soon begins to get quite painful. The flaps also should not be too short, or the edge will continually catch the top of the rider's boot, which is very uncomfortable.

Ladies' saddles require as careful choosing as a man's saddle, for the length of seat must suit the rider; and also the position of the crutches must vary in the same ratio. It is only a personal trial that is really of avail when selecting a saddle.

Stirrups should give a good broad hold for the feet; and then if the heels of the boots are brought well forward, ending in a line with the front of the leg, the top of the stirrup will always be kept clear of the tendon at the bend of the foot and leg, just above the upper spur-strap, which is otherwise apt to get very sore, when the foot is rammed well home. The hoop of the stirrup should expand into a broad wing on each side, where it joins the foot-plate, which saves the side of the foot from getting chafed. Stirrups must be wide enough for the boot to enter very easily, or there is a danger of the foot jamming in the stirrup in the event of a fall. On the other hand, they should not be too large, for fear the foot should slip right through, and so become fixed. Being dragged by the stirrup is a terrible danger, and every precaution should be taken to prevent such a calamity. Ladies should invariably use a safety stirrup, that will disengage their foot as soon as pressure is applied elsewhere than the foot-plate. It is a mistake to have stirrups so light that it is very difficult to get the feet into them again, if they should slip out when galloping or jumping. A moderately heavy stirrup is then much easier to catch with the foot than a very light one is. What also facilitates this operation is to take the stirrup into the hand before mounting, and after twisting the leather round twice, to give two or three sharp jerks to the stirrup, which will cause the leather and the stirrup to hang at nearly right angles to the saddle instead of being parallel to it. The quickest way, however, to recover the stirrup, and most sure, is to bend over, when galloping fast, and seizing the stirrup-leather close to the stirrup, place the latter on the foot with the hand. Even when steeple-chasing there is plenty of time to do this, and still to sit up again, and get your horse balanced for the approaching fence.

When at the covert-side in a country where a good run may be confidently anticipated, it is

most necessary to be on the alert to get away on
good terms with the hounds, for if a large field is
out, and you are unfortunately so far away that it
is impossible to get a clear course at once, the run
may be more than half over before it is possible
to extricate yourself from the crowd.   Then it is
that a horse with an extra turn of speed is so
useful ; and it must be made the most of to
catch up the pack, after which the horse will
probably not be extended to that degree that he
will be unable to get his second wind.   Hounds
very seldom indeed keep up such a continuous
pace that those actually with them do not get
plenty of opportunities to get an " easy," such as
never occurs in riding a steeplechase ; but those
who are struggling to get up to them, and are still
two or three fields behind, get no such welcome
chances, and have to keep galloping on without
any rest.   It pays better, therefore, to put on a
spurt at starting and reach hounds as soon as
possible than to keep toiling on some distance
behind.   Whether, however, it is possible to carry
out this plan without taking too much out of your
steed can only be decided by the circumstances
of the moment.

Careful watch must always be kept on the
leading hounds, and if they hesitate and drop
back into the pack, be prepared for a sudden turn,
or a check.   It is always well to keep on the
down-wind side of the hounds, for a fox turns
away from his line as often by hearing, or smell-
ing danger, as by seeing it ; though sometimes
what is likely to head the fox, such as a man
ploughing, may be discerned some distance ahead,
down-wind of his line, and as then he will have
to turn up-wind when he notices the man, it is

well to be ready for this contingency and edge off to that flank ; and the more so, for on turning up-wind the scent will probably improve, if the hounds turn with the fox without any check, and the pace will be faster than ever.

If it is certain there is no wire or other lurking danger, it is not necessary to almost pull a horse up when nearing a fence and then set him going again, as so many ordinary hunting riders do, even when hounds are running their best. It shows that the rider has not yet fully mastered the art of riding, and it loses a lot of time. If a firm, steady pressure is taken of the bit when about a hundred yards away, with an extra pressure of the knees, while the eyes are fixed on the exact spot selected, and not allowed to wander, the horse will instinctively go for that precise spot, and cocking his ears, will quicken his pace and judging his distance to a nicety, will sail over in his stride, with the least possible effort. It is most necessary to keep the same pressure on the bit, and to ride at the very twig first chosen, for if there is any hesitation on the part of the pilot the horse loses confidence, is at a loss what to do, and disaster may be the result. It is such vacillation that makes hunting men, who have had no practice in going fast at their fences, so dreaded by jockeys in a steeple-chase, for they will change their minds two or three times as to where they will jump, and the consequent wavering of their horses interferes with those on each side of, and behind them, and is a source of danger to all in their vicinity. Bold riding, with discretion, was formerly the safest way of crossing a country ; for when a horse has plenty of pace on, and is yet collected and well balanced, it is extraordinary what a distance of ground he can cover in his stride, if only he has a bold heart. A shrinking craven brute, that always stops when a ditch is before him to look "if there is sixpence at the bottom of it"—as that splendid rider the late Mr. "Fluffy" Robinson used to describe it—is no mount for a first-flight man! Alas, that free style of riding is almost a thing of the past! For unless possessed of such local knowledge that the hidden secrets of every fence are known, the dread of barbed wire induces a cautious manner of riding, that formerly was quite unneeded.

"A good horse never falls" is an excellent maxim to bear in mind; and it is indeed astonishing how extremely rarely a really good horse ever comes quite down. He may apparently be trapped over and over again, but he always has a leg to spare, and rights himself after a vigorous scramble. A horse that comes down more than twice or thrice in twice as many seasons should never be retained in a first-class stable. There is something wrong with either his conformation or his intelligence.

Different fences naturally require riding at in a different way, and a steed that knows how to adapt himself to all, and understands how to do them, is a treasure indeed. Timber requires careful handling, and should not be raced at, unless there is a wide drain on the further side, or much ground has to be covered. A firm hold should be taken of the bit, and the horse collected well on to his haunches, if the timber is strong and high. My own practice has ever been to ride as close to the post as possible, from the belief that this makes it easier for the horse to correctly gauge the height.

A horse trained to jump timber will be sure to jump walls, but the reverse of this is by no means the case. A careless wall-jumper is unsafe at timber, and the trick of taking off the top stones does not pay when applied to an unbreakable fence.

Wide water should be ridden at at a good pace, with a firm hold of the horse's head. Within reason, the firmer he is held the further he will jump. To see wide drains jumped properly it is well to visit the Ward Union district, round Fairyhouse, near Dublin. The fields there are divided by wide, very deep ditches, mostly dry, but their width and depth make them most formidable obstacles. They vary from twelve to sixteen feet wide ; and some are deep enough to contain both a horse and his rider, without it being even possible to see the latter's hat, while still mounted. The *habitués* of the hunt do not ride very fast at these obstacles, but at a steady hand gallop, giving a horse time to measure his ground so that he can take off at the very edge, and thus reduce the width as much as possible. In most English hunts, if there is any choice in the matter, it is common to see men ride at a wide ditch where there is a fence in front of it, " to make the horse rise," they say ; but a Ward Union man would never dream of doing such a suicidal thing. He would pick out, a spot where there was no hedge, so that the horse, by merely extending himself, can cover the width with the minimum of exertion. The best horse that ever was foaled would soon be beaten, if he was asked to go on jumping ditch after ditch in the Ward country, with a high fence in front of each. Much time and care is expended in teaching horses to jump these ditches properly, a pupil being made to jump moderate-sized ones backwards and forwards, perhaps thirty or forty times, till he will jump them in a skimming fashion, without rising into the air at all. So long as he essays to jump as if there was a small fence in front, he must be kept at it, until at length he will gallop and take it in his stride, keeping his head level, not dropping it in the least to look at the ditch, nor rising at all into the air. When hunting in that country, if some one is descried riding at a hedge in front of a ditch, it is a common remark to hear made, " Halloa! there's an Englishman." Every one within hearing will then turn in his saddle to watch the performance, for the mere fact of not riding at a ditch where it is open at once betrays a stranger to the practised eye.

When riding at water, the most important thing is to pick out a firm take-off, and sound ground preceding it for at least several strides. If the ground is treacherous it is impossible for a horse either to time himself properly or to make a vigorous spring, and to obtain such an advantage a little extra width to be covered may well be ignored.

Almost equally important is a firm landing place, and if this happens to be a trifle lower than the take-off it is an advantage ; for in open ground the horse can note there is a drop, and prepare himself accordingly. The contrary is the case when a hedge screens the landing from view, and the difference in level of only two or three inches is quite sufficient to bring many horses to grief, when racing over fences at their full stretch. A horse then expects the ground on either side of the fence to be the same level, and when the pace is so great he has no time to prepare himself should it prove otherwise.

It is usually safe to ride close to thorn-bushes, for such do not love wet ground, and the take-off will therefore be sure to be sound. Willows, on the contrary, should be avoided, for the soil is apt to be washed away from their water-loving roots, and a deep hole to be formed, a sure haunt for a big trout if there are any in the stream. As a rule it is safest to jump where the hounds have crossed, if the course of the stream is unknown, and there is no time to look before you leap, for a fox which knows the country is almost certain to cross at the narrowest spot, and if some of the hounds are seen to jump it clean, there is no doubt about a good horse being also able to clear the water. Even if hounds are seen to make a big effort to spring over, a horse will probably get over safely, for if the hounds feel it is too wide for them to leap, and that they must swim, they will just blob in, without making an effort to jump.

Often, when galloping, some deep ground—a slough of despond—is suddenly noticed just as the horse is about to stride into it, when the rider should at once lean back as far as possible, to throw his weight on to the horse's hind-quarters; otherwise a bad blunder, and possibly an over-reach will ensue; and if going very fast a strained tendon is not an uncommon result.

In the event of having to ford an unknown stream, take careful note of the soil of the banks, and character of the current. Where the stream broadens out over a gravelly or sandy bed, without any banks on either side, and with a babbling current, it is sure to be safe to ford it ; but beware of a loamy soil, or where there is a rapid current in a part only of the stream, between high banks, for though a portion of the bed may be firm, it may suddenly deepen, or be bottomless in mud. Rocky streams usually have many fording places, but gravelly spots must be selected; and it is often the case that the spit of gravel runs in a slanting direction, and not straight across, so caution must be exercised accordingly. It is never safe to plunge into a limestone river without local knowledge, for it is apt to be full of abrupt fissures ; and while one moment the water is quite shallow, the next step may be into excessively deep water. Before entering a stream be sure that the way out on the other side appears plain before you, for it is not always easy to retrace your steps on horseback.

There is one hint, learned many years ago in hot countries, that is most useful : never allow your horse to quench his thirst when entering a stream, but always make him cross about three-quarters of the way before doing so, whatever the width of the ford. The reason is that, if the animal is allowed to drink at once, he is likely to lie down suddenly without any warning, and roll, and some ludicrous scenes have been witnessed in consequence of the neglect of this precaution. If, however, he is forced to proceed nearly to the far side before drinking, he is so apprehensive that he is going to lose the opportunity, he eagerly drinks when given the chance, and thinks not about rolling. Horses are very fond of this amusement, and some will do it under the saddle. This most often occurs through their being girthed uncomfortably tight, when they roll from the natural instinct to rid themselves of the discomfort. It is especially liable to occur with ladies' horses, as it is at all times necessary to girth them tight, to prevent the saddle from shifting its place. As a man's weight is more evenly distributed, it is not necessary to draw the girths so tight, while if the saddle should slip back, a breast-plate will correct this tendency.

A horse seldom hurts himself by a fall at water, and very often clings for a second with his fore-legs on the further bank, before he rolls over, giving an active man time to spring off in safety. A lady has but small chance of doing this, as she cannot so quickly extricate herself from the hindrances of the stirrup and pommels. In a ditch country it is certainly an argument in favour of ladies riding on a cross-saddle. In a deep ditch the rider sometimes gets pinned under the horse, and is utterly unable to move, and is then in great danger of being badly injured by the animal in its struggles. If it is impossible to extricate the rider before the horse can be moved, especially if his head is in proximity to the animal's hoofs, a saddle should immediately be taken off another horse, and placed over the unfortunate man's head, to shield him from blows and kicks; and such a precaution may easily save him from disfigurement or even death. It is often difficult to get a horse out, if he is wedged on his back, and very probably digging will have to be resorted to. A great deal of assistance can be given him, in his endeavours to help himself, by pulling at his tail, or even his head, and no injury will be done if it is remembered to pull the tail either straight, or sideways; while the head must never be raised above a straight line

with the neck. If the tail is bent backwards it is
quickly broken; while the neck is easily dis-
located if the head is bent upwards. A horse
may be almost dragged out by the neck after a
rope has been placed round it, if only the pull is
in a straight line.

If the horse is lying on his back he must be
pulled over, and it is usually safer to pull him
over by the tail than by the head; for in this
case as soon as all the weight is on the haunches
some bone is very likely to break, either in the
thigh or the hind-leg. If, however, the horse is
lying on his chest, with a fore-leg doubled under
him, which is a common position, every effort
must be made to get the fore-leg pulled out, and
placed in front of him, for until both the fore-legs
are well in front, he cannot possibly rise. As
soon as his fore-legs are in the right position, he
should be threatened with a hunting-whip, and
even hit if necessary; for unless he makes a big
effort at once, which is almost certain to succeed,
he may lie there for hours, and becoming incapable of making a struggle, may succumb from
exhaustion.

If a rider is not seen to rise up again, when a
fall takes place, it is most imperative that any one
near should gallop to his assistance at once, for it
may make all the difference between life and
death, whether help is forthcoming immediately.
The good Samaritan, on reaching the spot, should
however, take measures for securing his own
horse, especially if the two riders are quite alone,
for it may be he will have to ride off for assistance, and if in his haste he has allowed his horse
to go free, much valuable time may be lost in
catching him again. There is no better plan than

one which was taught in my childhood, when beginning to hunt, nearly half a century ago. The reins should be pulled over the horse's head, passed through the throat-lash (which prevents the animal from treading on them while grazing), and then, after passing them under the fore-leg, tied to the stirrup sufficiently tightly to bend the animal's neck slightly down. The effect of this is that though the horse can move about, and also graze, he cannot raise his head to trot, without catching himself under the elbow, and therefore seldom gets far away, and is easily caught. If, however, it is done carelessly, so that the horse can straighten his neck, he can gallop off if he chooses, as if quite free. The success of the method depends upon the amount of bend given to the neck. The writer has many a time in wild countries tied up his horse in this manner in the middle of enormous flat plains, and then gone away for hours to shoot, and on his return found the animal close to where he was left. There is a knot, however, that it is necessary to learn, or the reins will come untied, for stiff leather is an uncanny thing to tie knots in. Fortunately it is a simple knot, and easily remembered. After passing the end of the reins through the stirrup, and adjusting them to the right length, shorten them by about another inch (as a little of the length is always lost in making the knot), and then taking *two turns* round the first two fingers of the left hand, pass the end of the reins through the loops thus formed, and draw all as tight as possible. If properly made, this knot never works loose.

When jumping hedges and ditches, there is less likelihood of a fall, when your horse is getting

17

beaten, if the ditch is towards you than when it is on the other side. A tired horse will generally manage to wriggle through the hedge somehow after jumping the ditch, when he would blunder into the ditch on the far side after jumping the hedge. Also it is a wise plan, when riding at a hedge with a wide ditch on the far side, to select, if possible, a gap in the hedge, or else a place where the fence is only a moderate height, so that the horse will see the ditch in good time before he makes his spring. Most backs are broken by a horse making an involuntary extra effort at the last moment on coming suddenly on to unexpected danger, when he had prepared himself for something quite different, the muscles of the back snapping the bones composing the vertebræ. Once at a race meeting in Ireland the writer saw no less than three horses crack their backs in different races at the same fence when leading. It was a ditch, and so concealed that no warning was given to the horse that it was there, and coming unexpectedly upon it, each broke its back. The horses behind escaped, for when they saw the leader suddenly make a jump they naturally were on the look-out for danger.

When riding at a ditch towards you, if it is very blind, try to choose a place where the ditch can be plainly seen, for then the horse can gauge what is before him. If this cannot be done, ride at a high part of the hedge at a good pace, so that the horse will have to stand well away to clear the obstacle. If you go slowly the horse will probably get too close, and getting his fore-feet into the ditch will give you cause to think over this hint !

Banks vary immensely in character, but all

require time for a horse either to change his feet on the top if it is broad, or kick back if it is narrow. An Englishman is apt at first to sail gaily down to a "narrow-back" and to charge it as if it was a flying-fence in his own country, but an Irishman treats it with great respect, especially if it is on the margin of a bog. Such banks are made of very crumbling material, and none require more training and cleverness on the part of the steed. A great broad bank, such as is often met with in Westmeath, for instance, which strikes terror into a stranger's heart, is treated by a native with much nonchalance, for they are very simple, if a horse is not in a great hurry. Banks that are covered with gorse, into which a horse must blindly plunge, are necessarily awkward obstacles, for much has to be taken on trust! Very formidable obstacles, too, are those in Cornwall and South Devon, on account of their perpendicular character ; while sometimes they are not less than eight or nine feet to the top, on which grows a luxuriant hedge. They are faced with stones for about four feet, to prevent bullocks horning them down, and a horse must dig his hind hoofs into the bank above the stones to get sufficient purchase to make another effort to get to the top. When he has got there it is quite likely there is an impossible place on the other side, and he must then turn round and come down the same way he went up. Possibly some of the most awkward banks to be met with are in the north of 'England, where, though the bank itself is not so very high, there is a playful custom of erecting a low post-and-rail on the top, to prevent that very active animal, a black-faced sheep, from trespassing into a neighbour's field. This is too formidable a fence to fly, while the bank is so narrow there is very little foothold for a horse to land on the bank and then screw himself over the rails. Good bank-jumpers from Ireland, or from the Blackmore Vale are quite nonplussed by such erections. They seem to say to themselves, "What on earth is this! I know all about banks! But what is this rail doing here?" They then proceed to chest the rail, and their arrival in the next field is usually in an ignominious fashion! It is wise to do a little private schooling at home before attempting to jump in public fences a horse is not accustomed to. In this case it is well to place the trunk of a tree on the top of a bank, and lunge the horse over this until it quite understands what to do, and how to do it. After it has learned this first lesson, a small rail may be substituted for the tree trunk, when the pupil should soon be perfect at rehearsal, and ready for crossing the natural country.

A " double " in Ireland signifies a bank with a ditch on each side; and though it is a formidable-looking fence, it is a safe one for a bold horse, when both the bank and surrounding ground are sound. It is different in boggy parts, when the foothold is treacherous. The writer once broke some ribs at one of these in rather a curious way. The mare made a bold spring, but the take-off being very soft, she did not get to the top of the bank, and while she was clinging to it, before falling back, there was time for the rider to fling himself out of the saddle on to the bank. Just as he had done so, and appeared to be safe, the mare fell back, and as she did so struck him with her head, knocking him off his perch to the bottom of the ditch, in an ungainly heap, two broken ribs being the result.

There was further reason to remember that day, for being near the end of the run it seemed as well to see it finished before going home, and the hounds checking directly afterwards, the writer happened to look at the thatched roof of a cottage, and there was the fox looking down upon the busy scene around him.

The old " double " at Punchestown is so well known that it may be interesting to many to know the exact dimensions ; they are therefore given as they existed when the writer won the Conyngham Cup with Belmont ; and probably there has been little alteration in them since. It may be pointed out that the bank in the " new double " —as it was then termed—in the Conyngham Cup course, was considerably higher, but being out of sight of the stands was not nearly so well known.

Ditch on take-off side	6 ft. 6 in. wide, 3 ft. deep.
Height of bank above the take-off	2 ft. 8 in.
Height of bank above the landing	4 ft.
Width of bank on the top ...	6 ft. 6 in.
Ditch on the landing side ...	4 ft. wide.

When riding at a fence uphill, it is very necessary to quicken the pace for the last stride or two and send the horse at it with a will, or he may not have sufficient impetus to get clear over, especially if there happens to be a ditch on the far side of the fence. From the natural lie of the ground, the animal cannot help being poised in a favourable attitude for making a spring. The contrary is the case, however, when going at a leap downhill, when a horse must be well collected and held together, and not hurried, to allow him to make his effort under favourable circumstances. If a horse catches hold of his bit, and goes with his head on one side when put at a fence, slacken the reins altogether for two or three strides till he has straightened his head, and then catch hold of him again, as otherwise he will jump on one side of the selected spot, and may come to grief.·

Q. What should be the guide in adjusting the length of the stirrups ?

A. The length of the stirrups for a man depends upon the conformation of each horse more or less, for the stirrups will require to be let out or taken up a hole or two, according as the animal is wide or narrow between the knees ; while the same animal may require the stirrups to be altered at different periods, on account of it being fat or thin in condition.

When about to mount, a good rough guide to the right length is to place the tips of the fingers against the stirrup bar, and then adjust the leather so that the bottom of the stirrup just touches the armpit when the arm is at full stretch. Though it may be necessary to alter the length a hole afterwards, it is at any rate certain that this length will allow of an excellent firm seat, which may be of much value in the case of a very fresh horse. Gentlemen fall into the habit of using faulty lengths, probably from being started in boyhood on a quiet pony that can be ridden any-how, and also from no one being careful to see at the very beginning that the child's stirrups are a workmanlike length ; a habit once formed is very difficult to alter.

Almost all professionals, such as whips and huntsmen, and also horse-breakers, ride with the same identical seat and length of stirrup, for they have had to take chance mounts from the beginning, and are therefore taught in a practical manner to sit prepared for any vagaries their steed may display.

Q. Can you describe this position ?

A. The stirrups are shortened sufficiently to bend the knee enough to get a firm grip with the inside of the knee-joint and upper part of the leg, the heel being kept down and back, so that if a line was dropped from the point of the knee it would just touch the junction of the foot and leg. Such a position ensures the rider being prepared for anything a horse may do, such as rearing, bucking, shying, kicking, or stopping suddenly dead in his tracks. Some evil-disposed horses can change from one malpractice to another marvellously quickly, and unless the balance is perfect, the rider must be unseated, for no grip can avail if once the balance is lost, and the horse continues his pranks. This length of stirrup can be gauged, when the rider is mounted, by letting the legs hang down to their full stretch, and then allowing the bottom of the stirrup to barely touch the upper part of the instep. When the foot is well home in the stirrup, the rider should be in a position to use his maximum power ; and since much of the weight of the body will rest on the thighs, it is well distributed to the advantage of the horse.

Q. What evil consequence is likely to ensue if the stirrups are too long ?

A. A powerful kick, or a series of them, may send the rider over the horse's head ; and a bad blunder at a fence may also cause the same disaster. The rider is also very liable to strain the inside muscle of the thigh, the "tailor's muscle" as it is commonly called, if a horse stumbles, or shies, or stops short suddenly. This is a most painful affliction, and not only takes some time to get right, but also leaves the sufferer quite helpless in the saddle, and barely able to keep his seat.

Q. What can minimise the ailment in some degree ?

A. It is possible to ride, and even to hunt, by wrapping a long soft leather strap round the afflicted thigh, in the form of a figure of eight, and then passing it round the body and fastening it by a buckle, much support to the injured muscle being thus afforded. These straps are made, and sold, on purpose for this treatment.

Q. What may happen if the stirrups are too short ?

A. If the horse rears suddenly very straight upright the rider is apt to slip off backwards, as he can get scant hold with his legs ; or else, by steadying himself with the bridle, he will pull the horse over backwards.

Q. What can a rider do if a horse rears badly ?

A. It is very seldom that a horse will come over backwards, if his mouth is not touched in the least, but as very little is required to make him lose his balance, the least clutch at the reins by the rider will very likely cause him to fall. If the rider is not taken unawares, and can at once press the heel of his left hand against the pommel of the saddle without taking hold, at the same time clutching the mane behind the ears with the right hand, when the horse rises up the rider will be lifted out of his saddle with him, and remain standing in his stirrups till the horse drops down again. Even if the horse should come over, the right hand holding on to the mane will keep the rider in such a position he cannot fall under the horse, the only thing likely to strike him being the horse's head. The writer is giving his own experience about this, as he has practised it successfully scores of times, without an accident.

Q. Should the rider stand up in his stirrups or sit down in his saddle when galloping?

A. He must certainly stand up, for otherwise he cannot give-and-take to the swing of the horse, as he passes over uneven or unsound ground, while his weight will be placed too far back. Weight is best carried by the forepart of the horse, but it must not be too forward, like in the exaggerated American seat. It is then put too much in front of the shoulders, on the horse's neck, the latter being the first part always to tire, on account of the great weight of the head, which is situated at the end of a long pole, so to speak. By the American seat this evil is much augmented by the rider's position, and besides allowing little control it does not afford any opportunity of easing the muscles of the horse by a change of position, such as from standing up in the stirrups to sitting down to finish. We all know what a relief it is when carrying a weight in one hand to change it into the other, and though the same weight is still being carried, for the moment it seems almost to have been quitted. No doubt a change of position is equally grateful to a horse when galloping.

Q. Should ladies ride with long stirrups or short ones ?

A. The stirrup should be a medium length. If a lady rides with a very long stirrup there is an advantage to the horse from her necessarily using the upper leg more in the trot, and consequently the stirrup, having less strain upon it, does not pull so much at the saddle, and there is less drag on the off-side of the withers. Her seat, however, is not so secure as with a shorter stirrup ; she must ride more by balance, through the left knee being straighter, and less aid is therefore obtained from the third crutch. It must be borne in mind that the more a lady throws her weight on the stirrup, the more likely she is to pull the saddle out of its place. With a very short stirrup also it is very difficult for a lady to sit squarely in the saddle, and she is almost obliged to ride in a twisted position, which is very ungainly.

Q. How should the reins be held ?

A. The reins must be separated, and one held in each hand, for it is childish to attempt to ride over a country with both reins in one hand. Each arm must be free and unhampered in its movements, or a considerable amount of power is lost. The elbows should always be kept close to the sides, for if they stick out at right angles to the body it is not only ungraceful, but power is also again diminished. A man sawing wood could not go on doing it unless his arm worked close to his body, backwards and forwards, and the action of pulling at a horse is much the same as the backward stroke in sawing.

The reins should, as a rule, be held at just such a length that the knuckles of the hands rest almost on the pommel of the saddle. They are then long enough to allow plenty of play to the horse's movements, and short enough to allow for considerable strength to be used, and are yet not so short that the arms cannot extend to meet a sudden peck, or snatch at the rein, when a very short hold of the reins might entail great discomposure of seat! Long reins are the foundation of fine hands; and this is partly the reason that ladies generally have light hands, as from the nature of their seat they must ride with plenty of rein. It is impossible for them to take their hold close to the middle of their horse's manes, as so many bad riders amongst men may be seen doing.

Q. What kind of bit can be recommended for cross-country work ?

A. The ordinary easy double-reined curb and bridoon, (in stable language termed a snaffle,) suits most horses' mouths, and most persons' hands sufficiently well, though it is often the cause of a horse dropping his hind legs into the further ditch, when a rider has become slightly unbalanced and seeks to steady himself by the reins. Some exceptional horses demand exceptional treatment ; and undoubtedly a horse will now and then give his rider less trouble in a bit that would drive other horses crazy. Many a really tender-mouthed horse is induced to pull extremely hard from being ridden in a bit that hurts his mouth so much that, in desperation, he summons up all his courage and, setting his jaws against it, pulls for all he is worth. By degrees the mouth gets hardened and deadened, and it will require much time, and great patience, to get him to carry his own head, and not hang on the riders' hands. A horse that bores, with his nose between his toes when galloping is best ridden in a gag-snaffle, for the peculiar action of this seems to make him raise his head, and go collectedly. It is needless to say a horse carrying his head so low is awkwardly circumstanced for jumping a high fence. Undoubtedly there is no bit like a smooth, plain, thick snaffle, but it must be associated with the finest of hands. The ordinary rider who pulls and hauls at a horse's mouth to convey his wishes and steadies himself with the reins when jumping will soon find that a free-going animal will require a very hard tug, before he can turn it, or stop it with a snaffle. It is not suggested that, even with first-rate hands, a horse will go pleasantly at once in a snaffle that is accustomed to the severer discipline of a curb bridle ; but he will gradually acquire a tenderness of mouth, responsive to the slightest indication, that can never be attained to the same degree with any sort of curb. The chief aim to be kept in view is never to put any pressure upon the bit without a definite object. The horse then learns to thoroughly understand his rider's wishes and, if a generous animal, will do his best to obey them. If a rider is constantly giving unmeaning touches and jerks to his mouth, the horse gives it up in despair, and has to be hauled at to make him obey by main force, when he really has not understood what was required of him.

The bit should at all times be just felt with a light, but steady touch. It is no sign of light hands, as some riders flatter themselves it is, to ride a not very keen horse with the reins hanging in festoons! Such a rider is not really in touch with his horse, and before he can give any indication of his wishes, must first commence by tightening his reins, thereby losing time. Indications given to the horse by the bit must at the same instant be supplemented with pressure by the legs, and a well-trained horse soon learns to interpret these so well that he might almost be ridden without a bridle.

A horse should never be ridden in a snaffle without a nose-band also, for if he chooses to open his mouth, he can render the snaffle of little effect. A nose-band just sufficiently tight to prevent the horse opening his mouth more than a very little, places the animal very much in the power of the rider, so long as his head is in the right place. Some horses learn that if they elevate their noses in the air they can force the snaffle to act only on the corners of the lips, and so get beyond the control of the rider ; and these have to be checkmated by using a martingale. Young raw horses also that go yawing about, and are difficult to steer, absolutely require the steadying influence of a martingale ; and it would be almost, if not quite, as great a handicap to ride such a one without a stirrup as in a snaffle bridle without a noseband and martingale.

Few grooms seem to understand the right length for a martingale, the usual custom being to have it so short that it only reaches a small way above the animal's chest, about in a line with the withers. This is certainly courting disaster, for though it is all very well to put it quite short in the case of a dangerous rearer, when riding over fences the rider might so hamper the horse, he would most likely make but a half-hearted spring. The right way is to hold the horse's head well up, and then so adjust the length of the martingale that the rings just reach the angle of the throat and head behind the jaws. This is quite sufficiently short to give great power in steadying, and controlling the animal ; while it does not fidget it at all, nor interfere with its comfort in any degree.

Martingales are also required for horses that have the dangerous habit of throwing back their heads, for a broken nose or concussion of the brain is no infrequent result of this most unpleasant trick. If the reins are merely passed under the jaws through two leather-covered metal rings, securely fastened together, the head can be prevented from reaching the rider's face without any martingale ; but a preferable plan is to use a standing martingale, usually termed a " Cheshire martingale," which terminates in two branching chains, with spring-hooks, that are snapped on to the rings of the bit. This does not interfere when jumping in the least, for if a horse is watched when taking a fence, it will be seen that the head drops somewhat, just as the effort to jump is made. It, however, effectively prevents the horse from tossing his head, and the first time he tries to do so gives such a wrench to his mouth, as much disconcerts him ; and very often a continuance of this plan eventually cures him of the habit altogether.

There is a snaffle which is a most valuable invention, for while it can be much more severe than a smooth snaffle, it is just as easy if a horse does not pull hard, and therefore the option lies with himself whether he is hurt or not. Moreover, all horses jump freely into it, and there is no fear of pulling a horse into a ditch when using it. It therefore suits many persons who find a curb bridle does not quite suit them ; while horses are not irritated by it, nor do they snatch at it, or throw their heads about when they are caught hold of (as the term is) to send them at a fence. These latter ways are most disconcerting, as it is impossible to make the most of a horse, or to do awkward jumps, if he will not allow himself to be steadied with the bridle ; and this is most usually caused by his being afraid of the bit. The great objection to chain and twisted snaffles is that they are always severe, and require a smooth one to be used in addition, to give ease to the horse when disposed to go quietly. This bit, however, combining as it does the severity of a twisted snaffle, and the ease of a plain one, is admirably adapted for using when a horse has been accustomed to a double bridle ; though it frequently happens that after some time his mouth gets so sensitive, that a further change may be made with advantage to a plain smooth snaffle. The bit consists of four smooth bars of steel, as if an ordinary snaffle had been sliced in half, and three large rollers inserted between each pair of bars, the whole constituting a " roller snaffle." When a horse is very headstrong, and determined not to stop, and the bit is drawn through his mouth, from side to side, all the rollers begin working, and few horses indeed will continue to rebel under this treatment. If, however, the horse does not pull, the bit becomes in effect a plain snaffle. Almost the only bits that have been used in the writer's stable for many years, for hunters, or steeplechase horses, have been roller, smooth, and gag snaffles, and there has been no necessity to employ anything else. There is indeed a double bridle in the saddle-room, regarded rather as an antique relic! It has been very seldom used indeed!

It has been mentioned previously that sometimes a horse learns the trick of getting his tongue over the bit, when the rider is powerless to control the animal if it chooses to go its own way. Some thirty years ago the famous Allen Macdonough, as fine a horseman and steeplechase rider as Ireland ever produced, invented, and gave to the writer, a " tongue-bit" which has proved most successful ; but it requires a nicety of adjustment an ordinary groom would hardly be likely always to attend to, and as otherwise the bit would not answer its intended purpose, and might easily be discredited, the particulars of it are not here stated.

Q. Should a rider let his body swing back as a horse rises at a fence ?

A. Certainly, and when exact time is kept it is much easier for the horse, as there is then no shock on his back when alighting. The rider should never rise a hair's breadth from his saddle the whole time, and the familiar " daylight" should never be visible. The hands also should be kept very low, and scarcely rise above the pommel of the saddle, moving forward as is required when the horse stretches his neck in taking the leap. The horse then gets the full benefit of his pace and spring, and is set going again the instant he alights. How seldom this is done in practice the sporting pictures that appear in the pictorial papers, done from actual photographs, most amusingly show.

Q. What are common faults in riding to hounds?

A. It is really dangerous when a front rider is suddenly afflicted with apprehension about the fence he is riding at—which is especially likely to happen if he is not used to cutting out the work—and thinking only of himself, pulls across others, who have already set their horses going at the fence, trusting that he will hold on the even tenor of his way. If the field have not yet settled into their places, it is pure luck if some one does not get a heavy fall, for even if all steer clear of the offender, and no one catches him broadside, and bowls him over as he deserves, some of the horses are sure to be thrown out of their stride in the confusion, and a heavy fall may be the result.

Other faults are far too common. There are riders who will not wait for their turn at a gate or gap, and others who shamelessly cut in before another at a fence ; and it is sad to say ladies are not free from these malpractices at the beginning of a run. At a later stage those who are still there are likely to know what they are doing, and to take care not to transgress against good manners and fair play. Those who behave in such ways would be the first to cry out, if a spirit of retaliation arose in the breast of their victims ! Another fault is that of following too close behind another at a fence, not making sufficient allowance lest the horse in front should

jump stickily, or refuse, or possibly fall. The
first two contingencies are only likely to occur
in the scurry at the start ; for no one in a hurry
would be likely to select as a leader any one
whose horse, or himself, was in the habit of
stopping to look before he leaped! The contingency of the pilot falling must, however, be
always kept in mind by the followers who honour
him by riding in his wake ; and the " length-and-
a-half " allowed by poor Fred Archer, in his
celebrated reply to the one who remonstrated
with him for not giving him sufficient room,
would scarcely be deemed enough by pilots in
general.

Q. Can any precautions be taken if a fall
appears imminent ?

A. If, in the course of a fast gallop, a fence
looks very forbidding, or one's steed has been
jumping so carelessly that it seems odds on it
falling when approaching a fence that must be
cleared to get over in safety, it is prudent to slip
the stirrups on to the toes, instead of keeping the
feet well home, so that if the horse falls the feet
will get clear of the stirrups at once, and the
dreaded danger of being dragged is thus
minimised.

When it is felt that the horse has made a
mistake, and is actually falling, the right hand
should be instantly pressed against the pommel
of the saddle, so as to push the rider away to the
left, when he will probably get clear of the horse
as they roll over together. The rider then falls
on his left side, with the left hand, that is holding the reins, towards the horse, and does not get
them torn from his grasp.

It is most essential to keep the eyes fixed between the horse's ears the whole time, when falling, until its head reaches the ground, for then the rider's body is instinctively prepared to meet the shock of the contact with the ground, and acts accordingly. If the eyes are looking elsewhere the rider falls in a heap, and the shock of the fall is exaggerated, as in the case of encountering an unexpected step in the dark.

When a run commences it is impossible to foretell how far off the end may be, and though the immense distances covered by stag-hounds are unknown in fox-hunting, the following valuable hints by Mr. Elsey may well be remembered :—

" Keep some wind in your horse, and beware of what you ask him to do if he is blown. Always ' suffer ' a little, and let your horse get a few easies if he is getting pumped, when he will recover his wind in a marvellous way. Even an easy for a few strides, helps a fit horse very much to recover."

When the necessity arises for putting into force such advice, it argues that the run has been both sharp, and far, and that the good horse has carried his rider safely to this point, while the end is approaching. Those who find themselves in such happy circumstances are fortunate indeed when the run has been

" Forty minutes on the grass, without a check, boys."

There are few more exhilarating moments in life than these.

APPENDIX

AN Order passed by the Department of Agriculture and Technical Instruction for Ireland came into force on July 1, 1906, prohibiting the landing in Ireland of horses, asses, or mules, brought from any port or place in Great Britain, the Isle of Man, or the Channel Islands, except under certain restrictions; and as this has escaped general notice, and much inconvenience may be caused by ignorance of the clauses, they are here stated.   The animals must be accompanied by

(1) A statutory declaration, made not more than three days before shipment, by the owner of the horses, asses, or mules, or his authorised agent, to the effect that the animals have not, within the preceding two months, been affected with glanders, or farcy, or parasitic mange, nor been exposed to the infection of those diseases; and

(2) A veterinary surgeon's certificate, granted not more than two days before shipment, to the effect that the animals were then free from the diseases above specified.

Before landing, these documents must be delivered to an authorised Inspector of the

Department, or the animals will not be allowed to disembark. The landing is also subject to such further veterinary inspection on behalf of the Department, as may be decreed by them.

After the horse, ass, or mule, has been landed under these conditions and has arrived at its destination, the person in possession, or charge of the animal, must forthwith give notice of the importation to the County Council (or County Borough Council as the case may be) of the district in which such place of destination is situated. The local authority may thereupon order such further veterinary inspection as they may deem requisite.

INDEX

UNWIN BROTHERS, LIMITED, WOKING AND LONDON.

THOMAS & SONS

beg to call attention to their

Novelties & Specialities

FOR HUNTING COATS, BREECHES, &c.

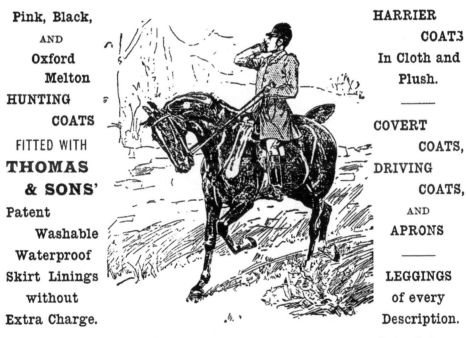

Pink, Black, AND Oxford Melton HUNTING COATS FITTED WITH **THOMAS & SONS'** Patent Washable Waterproof Skirt Linings without Extra Charge.

HARRIER COATS In Cloth and Plush.

COVERT COATS, DRIVING COATS, AND APRONS

LEGGINGS of every Description.

Masters of Hounds and Gentlemen waited upon in any part of the Country by appointment.

THOMAS & SONS,

Hunting Outfitters & Breeches Makers,

32, BROOK STREET, W. (Corner of South Molton Street.)

Telegraphic Address:
"SPORTINGLY, LONDON."

Telephone Number :
4652 GERRARD.

JOHN SIMMONS & SONS,

35, HAYMARKET,
LONDON, S.W.

HUNTING & HACKING HABITS.

SAFETY

SKIRTS.

INSPECTION
SPECIALLY
INVITED.
Patterns and Estimates
s-nt.

STRADDLE

SKIRTS.

FINEST HABIT CLOTHS ONLY USED.

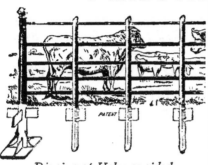
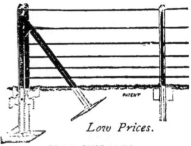
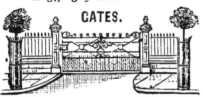
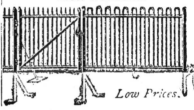

THE WALLET SERIES
OF HANDBOOKS.

A NEW SERIES OF HANDBOOKS, ranging over a wide field, which are intended to be practical guides to beginners in the subjects with which they deal.

Price per volume, in paper covers, 1/- net, post free 1/2; Cloth, 2/- net, post free 2/2; size, foolscap 8vo.

ON COLLECTING ENGRAVINGS, POTTERY, PORCELAIN, GLASS AND SILVER.
By ROBERT ELWARD.

WATER=COLOUR PAINTING.
By MARY L. BREAKELL.

ELECTRIC LIGHTING FOR THE INEXPERIENCED.
By HUBERT WALTER.

HOCKEY AS A GAME FOR WOMEN.
By EDITH THOMPSON.

DRESS OUTFITS FOR ABROAD.
By ARDERN HOLT.

THE MANAGEMENT OF BABIES.
By Mrs. LEONARD HILL.

ON COLLECTING MINIATURES, ENAMELS, AND JEWELLERY.
By ROBERT ELWARD.

MOTORING FOR MODERATE INCOMES.
By H. REVELL REYNOLDS.

ON TAKING A HOUSE.
By W. BEACH THOMAS.

COMMON AILMENTS AND ACCIDENTS AND THEIR TREATMENT.
By M. H. NAYLOR, M.B., B.S.

London: EDWARD ARNOLD, 41 & 43, Maddox St., W.

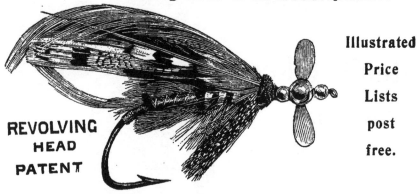

RIDING=HABIT OUTFITTERS.

Write for New Illustrated Booklet and Price List.

EVERY REQUISITE FOR COMPLETE RIDING OUTFITS.

Reliable Safety Skirts, Habits, Hats, Gloves, Stock Ties, Breeches, Silk Tights, Corsets, Boots. A Large Stock of Model Habits, etc , kept.

Save time and trouble by ordering at one establishment.

Speciality : The "Guterbock" Patent Ride-Astride Skirt.
Linen and Colonial Habits.

H. GUTERBOCK & SONS,

8. Hanover Street, Regent Street,

- LONDON, W.

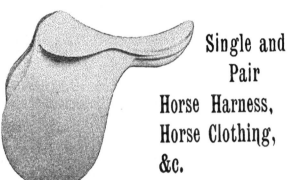

The Sportsman's Library.

EDITED BY THE

Right Hon. Sir HERBERT MAXWELL, Bart.

A Re-issue, in handsome volumes, of certain rare and entertaining books on Sport, carefully selected by the Editor, and Illustrated by the best Sporting Artists of the day, and with Reproductions of old Plates.

Library Edition, medium octavo, handsomely bound, gilt toos, 15/- a volume.

A SPORTING TOUR THROUGH THE NORTHERN PARTS OF ENGLAND AND GREAT PART OF THE HIGHLANDS OF SCOTLAND. By Colonel T. THORNTON, of Thornville Royal, in Yorkshire. With the Original Illustrations by GARRARD, and other Illustrations and Coloured Plates by G. E. LODGE.

THE SPORTSMAN IN IRELAND. By a COSMOPOLITE. With Coloured Plates and Black and White Drawings by P. CHENEVIX TRENCH, and reproductions of the original Illustrations drawn by R. ALLEN.

REMINISCENCES OF A HUNTSMAN. By the Hon. GRANTLEY F. BERKELEY. With the original Illustrations by JOHN LEECH, and other Illustrations by G. H. JALLAND.

THE ART OF DEERSTALKING. By WILLIAM SCROPE. With Photogravure Plates of the original Illustrations.

THE CHASE, THE TURF, AND THE ROAD. By NIMROD. With a Photogravure Portrait of the Author by D. MACLISE, R.A., and other Plates from the original Illustrations by ALKEN, and several reproductions of old Portraits.

DAYS AND NIGHTS OF SALMON FISHING. By WILLIAM SCROPE. With Photogravure reproductions of the original Plates.

London : EDWARD ARNOLD, 41 & 43, Maddox St., W.

Two Necessities for Hunting Gentlemen.

FINLAY'S Celebrated
RED COAT DRESSING.

Renovates old stained Hunting Coats equal to new! The best Dressing on the Market   **1/6** per bottle.

SLEIGH'S
SUPERIOR EMBROCATION.

Invaluable to Huntsmen! Cleanly to use. Rapid in action   One trial proves its merits.   **2/-** and **1/-** per bottle.

To be obtained through Saddlers and Harness Makers.

AGENTS EVERYWHERE IN THE UNITED KINGDOM

Wholesale ONLY from
SLEIGH & CO., Wholesale Saddlers
WALSALL.

Latest Testimony to the efficacy of FINLAY'S SCARLET COAT DRESSING.

Mr. ROBERT SMITH, Hunt Servant,
Angel & Royal Hotel, GRANTHAM,
writes under date Dec. 2, 1906 —:

"I can safely say if they will only give FINLAY'S SCARLET COAT DRESSING just one trial they will never use any other, for I have tried six different makers (and I can give you the names of them if you choose), and I will clean a scarlet coat, no matter how dirty or how old, with FINLAY'S SCARLET COAT DRESSING against any other maker's that can be brought before me.

"This is not idle talk, but from experience of years of cleaning scarlet coats. . . . I should like you to see the one that hangs up in my room now, envied by all the valets"

 If unable to obtain locally, please send for nearest Agent's Address to **SLEIGH & CO.,** Wholesale Saddlers, Walsall.

RYMERS

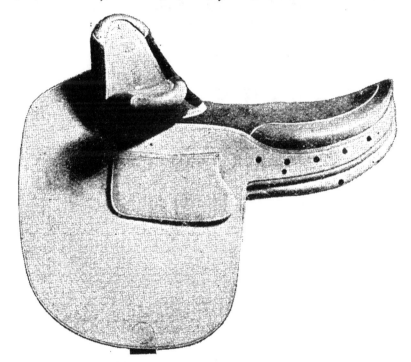